EMOTIONAL AND NARCISSISTIC PARTNER ABUSE

HOW TO STOP THE AGGRESSIVE NARCISSIST AND FREE HIMSELF FROM THE PSYCHOPATHIC PARTNER, TAKE BACK YOUR LIFE FROM A TOXIC RELATIONSHIP AND HEALING YOUR HEART FROM EMOTIONAL ABUSE

Table of Contents

Introduction

Once we enter a human space, we actively and unconsciously tap into and are affected positive and negative by the feelings of others around us. This natural propensity to in synch psychologically with the other people around us is what psychologists call psychological contagion.

Instinctively we respond to the emotional tone of those around us, and all ordinary people are, to some degree, susceptible to sensitive touch.

Mental contagion and empathy the most favorable form of the emotional disease is the foundation of human empathy virtue. We need to be in emotional harmony with others to comprehend, support, and function effectively in the human social world.

The compassionate observational skills of people make them more responsive than most to the nuances of the feelings of other people. It causes them sometimes to hate others because the mass of emotional signals is all too overwhelming. But even one-on-one relationships can be a challenge for a person to read and answer the subtle, sensitive questions of others.

As HSP's own emotional reactions are intense, rapid, and difficult to shake off, they often get caught in the feelings of others. Getting attuned to the rawness of other people's emotions, like emotional contagion, can be painful and upsetting.

The danger of Codependence Because unhappiness, frustration, or misery of others is so unbearable for someone with a high degree of sensitivity, and it is easy to understand why people would be tempted to cooperate and manipulate social situations in order to keep others emotionally equal. If the need to ensure that people around them never get angry or upset, there is a risk of developing mutual dependence.

Co-dependents feel accountable to others. We feel anxious when we learn about others who are suffering and do everything, they can to ease their burdens. The tendency of co-dependents to think about others impacts their own lives. It's easy for people who depend on others, but that leads to resentment. "Stay ahead of the other's emotional curve. Because a person with sensitivity can understand what others feel so emphatically and because they're often quite skilled at recognizing and naming feelings, they're sometimes in a peculiar position to have a person. The willingness to engage in direct and open discussion of difficult subjects is an essential communication skill, both as a quality and as a practice. It is easier to tolerate some of the distress you experience may be an emotional contagion arising in others instead of in yourself.

Chapter 1 What Is Narcissistic Abuse?

Energy protection is a critical competency for all people and a vital competency for coaches but is especially essential for those of us who are incredibly energy-sensitive. As coaches, we must consider our own energy system and make ourselves more mindful of the energetic interactions between us and our world and the people in it, and of course, the active exchange between ourselves and our coaching customers. This knowledge helps us to understand the forces with which we communicate every day and how they affect us and others in our surroundings. Nothing is as contagious as energy—we all influence each other across the full energy field, and if we understand the power of our energy, we will make better energy decisions for washing, refilling, and preserving our energy. When you feel exhausted after a customer interaction, there is probably an energetic explanation for this. Many coaches are also extremely sensitive to energy but do not know the flow of energy in their communications and coaching interactions. That is why the setting of boundaries is so important to us all.

Let me be specific; you have a private boundary structure, and you have been developing it for a lifetime. But it may be attached and ready to protect you like a smoke alarm or disconnected, suspended, or unable to warn you of danger by its wires. Without healthy boundaries, you can not thrive, and everything begins with you. You're doing what you love. When you understand where you stop, and others start, when you take full control of your life, become your best friend, you naturally establish better boundaries. Your border system describes you clearly, determines what you want, and won't allow in your life. You make conscious decisions for yourself. It lets other people know who they are, what they want, and what they can give.

Boundaries have three purposes: defending you, maintaining you, and encouraging your presence. And let me make it quite clear that you are not closed to life because boundaries actually allow you to feel safe to open up your field of energy. Borderline starting out with how you appear in your body, it starts off with signals that others take up in an intuitive manner — to begin by thinking about what you look like (hair, jewelry, clothes, shoes, conformity or non-conformity, trends, etc.) — the way you sound (words, speech patterns or laughs, tone).

Talk about what matters to you, your beliefs, your convictions. You always know when someone crosses a border because there will be an internal alarm. Your instincts and your conscience, your moral and ethical compass, your honesty, and your emotions are precious here. Being in your body will allow you to understand what is happening to you, and if you believe a limit has been through, decreased, or just frustrated. Tables. Lists.

Finally, how can you activate your borders when an alarm sounds and borders are challenged? What can you do? There was a mistake.

This helps clear agreements with others, so you have clarity about what is and will not happen, so that if an alarm sounds easy to remind you of your previous contracts. Trust yourself to defend your limits with words such as "No, that's not my style." "I am sorry I don't go in the direction I want to go to." Be clear about your commitment to your goals. And have your limits-think of the signs your presence is genuine and appropriate; step confidently to demonstrate an enthusiastic and yet calm awareness of your intention. If you do this, you and your energy will be trusted. You have to speak, though, to enforce the limitations, and I will talk to a stereotype for a moment-if you are woman, responsive, empathetic, you only hear me when you often say that no one can be a full word.

Boundaries are then the first energy protection level. And since I'm sure you can tell limits, self-awareness starts. You must learn yourself indoors and outdoors. Once you have discovered yourself more thoroughly and become aware of your own power, you will step into the second level of protection to defend and protect your life. You must be fully in your physical body to do practical energy work and influence energy around you, and you must feel that your body is firmly connected with the world. You must be able to breathe calmly, consistently—if you can't, then you tend to be inaccurate in your perception.

Let's take a look at yourself—three questions:

- Are you well-grounded?

- How much are you in your body?

- Is your breath rhythmic and calm?

Check-in and alert yourself. Trying to remain in them with a steady breath, they all really wanted to be confident.

Do your inner work and even know the enemy inside. Your side of the moon. Why because you sometimes get negative energy from outside, because an alarm sounds internally-sometimes those feelings are yours. I've had many customers try to avoid their own problems by accusing the energy fields of everything. Unpleasant, "bad" emotions are signs of the false. However, most people think this means something is wrong if the whole answer lies inside, and we project it onto other people. As coaches, we must be mindful of our predictions. It could be your thoughts, not anything outside of you. It can be a warning that you say flawed ideas to yourself if you have negative emotions. You're thinking the wrong way.

Pick up your thoughts. Order your thoughts. Replace thoughts, beliefs that make you feel less fulfilled with those that make you happier. This obviously means that it's not beneficial to hide your feelings, to stuff them inside you. It's all burying the problem. You must learn to understand what you feel, what you hear, and what thoughts these feelings make. You must then learn how to change perceptions because it is likely dangerous to focus on these negative emotions rather than to repress them! If you are living on negative emotions, you will attract them in your lives. Non-violent communication from Marshall Rosenberg is an excellent resource for learning how to recognize and transform your feelings.

Remember that your own portable space is your energy field-more than just an abstract range. It is an energy field that flows and surrounds you, an extension of your own feelings, mind, and spirit-it's your consciousness ' living force field.

Think about how much space you need physically around you, and how much energy do you start feeling when you communicate with others? You can expand and contract your energy field. In fact, you will probably do this unconsciously all the time.

Inside and outside, learn yourself. Love yourself enough to set clear limits.

Take care of yourself to do any energy work; you need to be balanced and in good health.

Get clear of your boundaries and put them into practice-not in a rigid manner but in a consciously flexible way, live with them and evolves when you find what works and what does not enhance your energy awareness, the energetic exchanges between yourself and others-play with your own personal space and protection techniques Be aware of the massive energy trapped, whether it's yours or someone else, and practice removing it. Your own energetic burden is essential. As a coach who is interconnected with the earth's energy field, you need to know what energy you feed into the world. Because every feeling, every thought you have, is a vibration, which is making in the world more of itself! And we've got sufficient negativity. You are a resonance force field.

Sensitive: can someone be overly sensitive to trapped emotions?

Several people are described as overly sensitive and empathic. And while this leads to many benefits, there are many difficulties as a result of this method. We can feel like sponges that absorb anything and everything in a setting.

For other people that are sensitive, but maybe not to the same degree, they can take everything to heart. One expression, look, or a lot of voice, and you can feel overwhelmed emotionally.

If the world was suitable for this kind of person, their lives would be much more comfortable. And yet, in many cases, it is best suited to people who feel enthusiastic and disconnected. Here you are not in touch with your feelings, let alone sensitive, and you can't feel them.

Therefore, even though both of these extremes are questioned, feeling dumb is more suited for today's world. This does not mean that it is absolute truth and that sensitive individuals have no position or can not succeed. What is usually concerned is the business environment and areas where people are out of touch.

In these kinds of environments, it is not always viewed as unusual to become emotionally cut off and to wear masks; it is often perceived as natural and as life is. On this basis, one could infer that being sensitive is a bad thing, and something must be modified in some way.

This could lead to some kind of personal harm, and one could feel a sense of shame for being like it. Because they don't suit the way most people are, they may decide that being like other people that are not responsive would be more comfortable. And while in some situations it may be better to be like people who are not so sensitive, there are many advantages one would miss.

One thing is to criticize oneself and another to receive criticism from others. You may obtain all sorts of tags from others, and if they are not sensitive, it would be easy; because they do not know how painful it is to be.

And if you have not experienced anything or are not very empathetic, you can hardly really understand what someone else is going through. Some things others could say: you are too sensitive; what they said was just a joke; you have to grow up; you shouldn't take things so personally; just let go of it and don't get it worked up.

Logic Now, these opinions that come from the mouth of another may sound logical and even support them, but that's all about it. If it were as simple as internalizing these beliefs and becoming less reactive, indeed, that would be the case.

But it's not so easy. So no matter what the mind of another person comes up with or what one feels of himself, it doesn't have to change something.

The Other Alternative Many people will be sensitive at one stage and eventually end up insensitive. And this can make them critical of vulnerable people. These people might remind them of what they refused, and perhaps they used food, alcohol, drugs, or some kind of muscular building to tone their sensitive side. So in most cases, they went from being extremely emotional to feeling very little.

Or you can go from one extreme to the next; sometimes, you feel extraordinarily reactive and sometimes. This could focus, for example, on what is happening in this person's life.

Examples For those who are excessively sensitive, it can affect all aspects of their lives or only specific areas. One could not deal with criticism from others, be it negative or positive, and be provided with the best of intentions.

Relationship breaks may be another area that wipes this person out and overwhelms them. Loud noises or large crowds in places full of people could be another boiling point.

Powerful, Loud, and regulated people may cause problems. You should do everything you can to stop any conflict or confrontation and find it difficult to stand up for yourself. Watching the news or living in the circumstances could be too much for people to manage.

Explanations Now, there will be as many explanations why someone is too sensitive. Next, the nervous system is different from someone who lives differently. One thing that can cause someone to have no control over their excitement is if their emotions and feelings are trapped.

And as they are trapped in your body, the nervous system can affect yourself and cause you to have a higher level of excitement, either at certain times or in the way of life. These could be adults and go home when you were a kid and an infant.

This could be because of an incident that was extremely traumatic or an accumulation of minor events that, for instance, caused pain. And since they stay in your body, you have very little say in how you feel; it is an involuntary reaction and not a conscious decision.

Awareness This is not to say that by releasing those trapped emotions and feelings, you lose your sensitivity. But it could mean that their enthusiasm would calm, and the nervous system reflects this transition. Therefore, even if one is still sensitive, they might not be too sensitive any longer. It could also lead to better limits to protect their delicate nature.

A psychologist or a healer will support you in this process, helping you to confront and relieve your feelings and emotions.

How cultural sensitivity and labeling affect people with intellectual handicaps

Cultural sensitivity is defined as knowledge of cultural differences. Getting mindful of these differences also has an effect on training and behavior. Examples of cultural sensitivity include attending cultural events or religious centers, changing the environment of the individual, or discussing life experiences in connection with the culture of the person. Labeling involves representing someone positively or negatively in a short word or phrase. For instance, the name of a person can harm the self-image, the categorization of a person without his permission, or indirect recognition in a group (using an incorrect term to describe an individual).

To staff, physicians, health professionals, and family members, cultural sensitivity and branding are critical to be aware of. It is essential to recognize the importance of a person's culture. Culture forms your personality and part of your environment; culture can even affect challenging behavior. It is also essential to recognize that diversity affects interaction and involvement. For instance, a person may not be used to be around different cultures or races. This is particularly true in view of the ever more diverse patient population in America and the health status differences between people of different ethnic, racial, socioeconomic, religious, and cultural backgrounds. An individual needs to respect differences in other people, including practices, behavior, opinions, beliefs, interaction styles, traditions, and institutions, to appreciate diversity. One of the significant components of cultural insensitivity and labeling can be the language barrier. For example, a person may speak in English but prefer to talk in Spanish or vice versa.

Active treatment, which also involves active participation, takes place when people are engaged in positive activities. Participation improves when both workers and individuals embrace cultural standards. Conversely, the belief that all members of an ethnic, linguistic, or religious group share a common culture is incorrect. The larger group can share everyday historical and geographical experiences, but individuals may share nothing in the group. The way a staff handles the actions of a person in a new environment is essential to the tolerance of culture — for example, an individual from another district, state, or even country. Adapting to your situation only helps you to feel more comfortable. The primary and most important aspect is education. Education. It is crucial that workers are willing to learn more about customs or characteristics of cultures to better connect with their individuals; not everyone was born or raised in the same place. Simple things like to learn a few Spanish words to better communicate with your Spanish speaker can go a long way.

One of the biggest hurdles in the implementation of person-centric planning is when people do not understand each other. Whether from a different race, ethnicity, or history, disabled persons deserve the same rights and opportunities that we have. Labeling can also be disrespectful and can destroy people's relationships. In addition, we as employees need to educate others about the acceptance of cultures. Person-centered planning takes place specific to the goals or goals of each individual. Engaging in more cultural activities increases employee knowledge and relationships.

There are many ways that a healthcare clinician, worker, and family member can communicate with a person in culturally sensitive ways. A cultural director, a staff member, or a clinician should see all patients as individuals and understand that their views, background, beliefs, and vocabulary influence their expectations of the provision of medical care, acceptance, and enforcement of a diagnosis. If you're from the West Indies, it won't be enough to coordinate community inclusion tours to local West Indian restaurants. It is imperative to maintain and develop a relationship with the family. Talk to the family what the person likes, what does he or she do for fun? How does he or she take part in family roles? Members of the support group should also understand their own cultural values and draw parallels where possible, listen to your people about past experiences, and how they grew up in a different country? What they miss? What they miss? Therefore, be aware of the fact that people can communicate in voice, language, or body language differently. Avoid labeling and refrain from saying' I don't understand,' and identify prejudices and stereotypes that prevent them from effectively communicating with patients from different cultures. One of the most critical mistakes that staff can make is to equate the religion of an entity to some person or another. Your guy, for instance, wants lunch at the Spanish Restaurant, but the staff says they don't like Spanish food because it is easier to have two fats, fried chicken and black-eyed peas! Think of the impact of this comment and how the person would feel if you judge their decision. However, he or she always has compassion for the individual. What if you were able to react to this, how would you react? How would you preserve your lifestyle? Open to everything!

The Psychometric Practice and Psychic Children

One of my skills as an empathic sensitive is the psychometry of artifacts. Like all spiritual gifts, this one allows the reader to acquire specific perceptions of emotions and thoughts. The stronger of the two cognitive systems, Emotions seem to get through a little more directly, but they can seem somewhat confused and disjointed. On the other hand, thoughts can be softer and simpler but can be a little harder to pick up if the person in question does not have a high level of focus.

The recipient must learn to become a passive recipient for psychometry to function. That is, he or she who reads should make every effort to release preconceived notions or expectations so that information is correctly received. Say, for example, giving you a costly watch. On the surface, you would think that the owner was somebody with great resources and a lot of money. This assumption is based on a social filter or expectation based on surface appearances, which could very probably be a false premise.

The best practice is to take the object instead of basing the readings on surface appearances without any implied representation. Enable the energy of the object to move without preconceived restrictions to prevent it from being modified. Even if you receive the power, try not to make any personal assumptions about the acquired images. After all, no one is entirely faultless, and, just as we want to be respected despite our faults, let him read the same courtesy.

It is, therefore, necessary for a reader to create a neutral point of reference for any reading. It is straightforward to establish a neutral reference point, but it can be one of the hardest tasks to accomplish successfully. As with meditation, with the exception of purpose, the same principles apply. In this scenario, you intend to find a position where you can neither control nor be controlled in a passive mode. When you come to this state, remember how you feel, so that later you can re-enter the country when necessary.

Chapter 2 What Causes Narcissism?

Narcissists are surprisingly hidden. They are masters at disguising themselves in public, blending in and working their manipulative magic behind the scenes. They do not want to be called out for what they are, and the majority of them take necessary effort to hide their abusive tendencies behind plausible deniability. Snide comments are disguised as jokes. Words meant to shatter you, demean you, and control you, are hidden behind a façade of concern for you or your wellbeing. The worst part is, people tend to fall for it. People inherently want to trust others, and they often will take other people at face value. They seek to take advantage of this, using it to continue to operate behind the scenes as they seek what it is, they truly want.

Identifying a Narcissist

When you are trying to identify a narcissist, you may as well be trying to prove the existence of something so sneaky that it will take some serious effort on your part. People around you probably deny that there is anything wrong with the person who has been abusing you, or they announce that you must be delusional. Because narcissists are so charming, so capable of identifying how they present themselves to others, and such good manipulators, you may find yourself on a wild goose chase if you do not know where to start or how to identify one. When trying to identify a narcissist, try the WEB method. WEB stands for Words, Emotions, Behaviors.

Watch their words

When attempting to identify a narcissist, the first step is identifying words or ways of speaking that are indicative of a narcissist. Their words typically take either extremely positive or negative connotations; they show a lack of empathy or they are manipulative words that paint the narcissist as a victim.

- Positive words: Positive words are used to draw in the narcissist's target. They will word things incredibly positively, seeking to hook the target to the narcissist and allow for future manipulation. These words can be seen as seductive, as they essentially seduce the narcissist's targets into submission. These are words like:
  - I love you so much!
  - You are the best person I have ever met!
  - Wow, you are so good at your job, and you deserve the world. Let me give you everything you deserve.
  - We will go to great places in this world if we stick together!
- Negative words: Negative words are a direct contrast to the positive. Negative words are used to disparage

or tear down the narcissist's target. These are typically weaponized to directly harm the target and browbeat the other person into submission. Negative words may look like:

o Wow, you are completely incompetent.

o You never do anything right.

o Look at that idiot over there—he didn't recognize the greatness in my proposal I made for the new job.

o You know, you could be a much better person if you'd only listen to me. Maybe you'd do something the right way for a change.

- Uninterested words: These words show a lack of empathy, or that the narcissist does not care about other people. He may halfheartedly listen to what is being said but shift the topic as soon as he has the chance to do so. Particularly if you are complaining about something that happened, the narcissist may voice how he had it worse. Any concerns or discomfort you may be feeling are disregarded altogether.

o Maybe you should have tried harder. I faced a similar situation, but I managed to get through okay because I actually tried.

- o Yeah, that sounds annoying, I guess, but it could have been worse. I had to deal with this before. Let me tell you how THAT was hard.

- o Okay. What do you want me to do about it?

- o I don't really care. Can you help me with this thing over here?

- **Victimizing words:** The narcissist sees himself as superior, just by virtue of his personality, and because he is superior, he feels he can only fail when he is an innocent victim of happenstance, and the failure had nothing to do with himself. The narcissist often uses words that will portray himself as the victim when talking to others, or even in his own internal monologue. He may say things like:

  - o That was so unfair. I should have been the one promoted for the job. Everyone knows I'm better than the other person anyway.

  - o That was not my fault! Someone else interfered. I would have been fine if they hadn't shown up.

  - o How could you do that to me? I didn't deserve that.

  - o Why are you trying to hurt me? I may have made a mistake, but look at how you responded! You're treating me so poorly.

Watch your emotions

The next step to identifying the narcissist in your midst, after listening to the words said, is to watch how you feel around him. If you feel like what the narcissist is saying is too good to be true, then it probably is. Even though at the moment, you may feel the greatest joy you have felt in a long while, particularly due to their long soliloquies about how much they love and cherish you, such a strong response may feel as though it could not possibly be real—because it is not.

If you find yourself feeling incredibly negatively about yourself, whether inadequate, unsuccessful, unworthy, or even anxious and as though you are walking on eggshells, you should look at the relationship closer. While everyone feels down about themselves sometimes, it should not be a regular occurrence. If you notice that your feelings seem to oscillate with the suspected narcissist's own word patterns, you should probably move on to the next step in trying to identify the narcissist.

Watch their behaviors

Paying attention to what the suspected narcissist is doing separately from what he is saying will help you identify whether he is a narcissist or not. Narcissists typically say lots of things in rapid-fire sequence in an attempt to keep you distracted from the problematic behaviors. This is a manipulation tactic—you are so focused on the words that you miss the abusive or insensitive actions happening right under your nose.

Particularly, you should pay attention to see if the narcissist is easily frustrated or angered when things do not go quite according to plans. Narcissists typically lack flexibility, and when they feel as though their control over the situation has been thwarted, they lash out at others. If the narcissist responds through snapping at you instead of rationally approaching the situation like an adult, you may have a problem. Likewise, if you noticed that the narcissist does insensitive things, such as taking a coworker's lunch out of the fridge or cutting in front of people waiting for a coffee, you may be able easier identify the narcissist.

Lastly, the narcissist has a tendency to blame others for anything that goes wrong. Watch to see if the suspected narcissist is constantly blaming other people even when everyone knows that the narcissist is the one who has made a mistake. This is a telltale sign of the narcissist.

Diagnosing Narcissistic Personality Disorder

Narcissists are not just people who are annoying to be around. True narcissists actually suffer from what is known as a narcissistic personality disorder (NPD), and it is a recognized mental health disorder that has a pervasive impact on the individual with the disorder and how he or she functions through life. Ultimately, the DSM-5 has identified several traits that are shared amongst narcissists. They must meet at least five of the nine presented traits to be clinically diagnosed, but even those who do not meet clinical diagnostic criteria may still be quite toxic to be around. Proceed with caution when you have identified a narcissist, as the traits he likely has can make it quite difficult to interact healthily. The traits of NPD all fall into one of three categories: A lack of empathy, an innate, insatiable desire for attention, and delusions of grandeur. The nine traits are depicted in the following graphic, as well as detailed, in-depth here.

Grandiosity

The most obvious of the traits is the grandiose nature narcissists everywhere seem to have. The narcissists believe that they are better than everyone else, and treat it as if it is an inherent fact, needing no more justification than any other inherent facts, such as the sky being blue or that hearts beat to keep people alive. The narcissist simply is better, stronger, smarter, faster, and generally superior to those around him. He believes that he is perfect exactly the way he is.

This belief of perfection then entails that the narcissist believes that he is infallible: He can never be at fault because perfection is never wrong. This means that he could never possibly be wrong because being wrong would deny his inherent superiority and perfection. He insists that everything he does is intentional and serves exactly the purpose he needs it to, or that some external, uncontrollable force sabotaged him. He did not fail due to a lack of skill, but rather because of happenstance, or because someone else messed up so badly that not even his perfection could save the situation.

Obsession with fantasies of power or success

Because narcissists assert that they are better than everyone else, they are preoccupied with the idea that they should have the power, success, status, and anything else they desire to prove it. Their perfection should go hand in hand with power and success, as far as they are concerned, and they obsess over obtaining it. The narcissist will do anything possible to convince others that he deserves it.

Unfortunately, the narcissist's own standards are unrealistic and oftentimes entirely unattainable for the average person. Very few people get to live the dream the narcissist has, and this means that the narcissist's beliefs of perfection and fantasies of power are constantly being challenged. This keeps the narcissist in a state of constant dissonance, in which he believes one thing but gets something entirely different. He struggles to accept this, and it often leads to denial, manipulation, and narcissistic rages.

Delusion of uniqueness

The narcissist, as a perfect individual with fantasies of power that he believes he has or should have, also believes that he is perfectly unique. No one is on par with him, and therefore, no one can ever understand him, his desires, or his logic. He will use this in two ways: It works to deny when people question his motives, as he can just assert that there is a method to his madness, and anyone who fails to see the method is simply too dumb to understand it, or he can use it to justify that the other person is not special like he is, and therefore is inferior in some way. If the other person is inferior, there is no reason to concern himself with the other person's belief as it is irrelevant and not at all educated. After all, if the narcissist is really so special and unique, he must be superior by default.

Because the narcissist is special and no one can ever understand him, he is also able to play the perfect victim. No one understands his plight, and no one understands how he suffers. This means that no one can dare judge him for his behaviors or criticize him because he has it so much worse than anyone else, and no one else understands how badly he feels. Never mind the fact that other people have likely been through incredibly similar situations, or worse, just through sheer numbers of people. Most likely, there is always someone who is in a worse state than the narcissist, though he will never admit that.

Further, the narcissist will use his uniqueness to deny any sort of relationship with people he deems as inferior. He will refuse to associate with people who do not relate to him and may even choose to only shop at certain stores, wear certain brands, or eat certain foods that align with his superiority.

The never-ending desire for attention and admiration

The narcissist seeks to constantly be inundated with love, attention, and admiration. He needs this to justify his own existence, and while he may not consciously feel as though his superiority needs justification, he does justify it in comparing himself to others, even if that justification is delusional in the first place. He craves the attention of other people and will do anything he needs to do to get it, whether it is manipulating others, forcing himself to be a victim, or inserting himself as the center of attention when he should not be. No matter the situation, the narcissist has a plan to ensure that he gets the narcissistic supply, the sort of mental energy sustenance that he requires to feel secure in himself.

Entitled

Entitlement naturally follows with the previous traits of the narcissist. He believes that he deserves what he wants simply because of who he is, and he never wants to put in the effort. He will expect other people to cater to his whims, or he may simply wait for what he wants to be brought to him on a silver platter. Regardless of how it works out, the narcissist believes that he deserves it all with none of the work.

He expects to win despite having never proven he is skilled at whatever he is doing. He expects the promotion he does not qualify for. He expects to get the girlfriend he wants without putting in the effort or recognizing that she has free will and can decide whether she likes him or not. He expects the house, the prestige, the money, the power, and the general success at all of his endeavors simply because he deserves it. He believes he should have it, and that is enough.

Manipulative and exploitative

Narcissists do not perceive the world the way normal people do. They see everything through a distorted perception of reality, and they believe that their distortions are the truth, no matter how much people may point out that they are mistaken. The narcissist then feels as though he has to force everything around him to line up with his skewed perceptions, and he will manipulate others in order to browbeat them into line. He will gaslight others, believing the words that come out of his mouth so thoroughly that the other person begins to believe them too. He will tell people that they are incompetent, inferior, undeserving, or generally at fault because he believes it, and he will manipulate the listener into believing it as well. He will disguise himself with a persona in order to make himself seem more desirable and to exert the aura of perfection he believes he has in order to manipulate others into believing his reality. When people do not bow to his demands and see the world through his eyes, he will choose to instead threaten or exploit them into obedience instead. The manner he manages to get what he wants is of little consequence to the narcissist, so long as he ultimately gets his way and his delusions are upheld.

Lacking Empathy

Narcissists lack basic empathy. They are unable to really relate to how others are feeling, and because of that, they struggle to care about how other people are doing. They do not feel motivated to stop harming others, even when their behaviors are destroying another person. They do not care enough to feel guilty about the manipulation tactics they use. They do not see a reason to meet other people's needs. All of these behaviors lead to an individual who is not suited for life in a smoothly running society. The narcissist seems to go against the grain when in social groups, stepping on others and using them to his advantage rather than creating a way for everyone to benefit. The only person he cares about being successful, happy, or cared for is himself, and every action that he will do will be in his own interest.

Envious of others, while also believing others are envious of the narcissist

The narcissist frequently envies other people, particularly if they have what he wants. They may have worked hard for what they have, but the narcissist does not care. The narcissist wants to get it too but expects to have it handed to him. He instead wallows in his own envy of the other person before eventually twisting it around in his own mind, changing the narrative into the other person envying him instead. For example, if he looks enviously at someone who has managed to get a promotion, he may then tell himself that he did not want the job anyway, and that the other person will be jealous when the narcissist is on vacation and getting off work on time every day while the other person attends to newfound responsibilities that came with the promotion.

Arrogant

Due to their beliefs of superiority and uniqueness, the narcissist frequently separates himself from people that he sees as beneath him. He frequently comes across as arrogant to nearly everyone because of this haughty demeanor he uses when asserting his superiority. He only bothers showing any signs of respect to people who are equal or superior to him, and so few meet that standard that he has set that he frequently just comes across as arrogant to all.

Chapter 3 Who is The Narcissist?

One of the most difficult things for victims of narcissists is learning to let go. When someone is dear to you, it is normal to see the best in them. You try to get them help, try to understand them and hope that someday they will change. Unfortunately, this is not always the case.

Narcissists do not seek help. They believe they don't have a problem. If anything, in the mind of a narcissist, the person who thinks they need to change their ways is the one who needs to embrace change. It is so traumatizing, watching someone you love dive deeper into the abyss like that.

If you cannot change someone, at best you can learn how to cope with them. Remember that in as much as you might hold them dear, your first priority is your personal safety and peace of mind. In learning how to handle a narcissist, you can counter their manipulative motives and prevent yourself from becoming a puppet.

The first step is to learn how to identify a narcissist, which we have done. Next, you learn how to identify their manipulative traits, and what to do in order to counter their outbursts. In a relationship, it is very difficult when you realize you are living with a narcissist. The best solution is always to keep a healthy distance from a narcissist, especially if you know they can overpower your resolve.

Four-point framework for dealing with a narcissist

There are several ways of handling a narcissist. Before we look into them, the following are four of the most important things you should always keep in mind when dealing with a narcissist.

1. Positivity

Life throws many curve balls at you all the time. It never gets easier. To get through anything, you must embrace positivity and change your outlook about life. Narcissists will drain the life out of you, and by the time they are done with you, all that's left might be a shell of your former self.

People who maintain a positive approach to life generally live happier lives than most. Your happiness is one of the things a narcissist will go after. When you are happy, to them it means there is something else in your life responsible for your happiness, something other than them. Since your life must revolve around them, they will do everything they can to take away your happiness.

Narcissists will do random things to disturb your peace. They also monitor you to see the effect. It fills them with joy when you lose focus and are disturbed. They respond by pushing your limits further until you break.

Staying positive will help you learn how to handle a narcissist. They have an endless barrage of insults and ill behavior that they can hurl at you. Instead of bowing to the pressure, be positive and show them that you are not affected by the things they do or what they say. If you are persistent, they might soon realize that it is impossible to break you, and they have to make peace with it.

Positivity is not just about handling a narcissist, it is also about your mindset. You need to stay sharp because a narcissist will never give up on testing you. You can condition your mind to think positively, filter negative vibes and focus only on things that bring joy, meaning and satisfaction in your life. This will help you become aware of, and impervious to narcissistic manipulation.

2. Healthy boundaries

One of the top recommendations when dealing with a narcissist is to set boundaries. This helps, especially when you realize you are in an unhealthy relationship. The challenge with setting boundaries is that in most cases, people don't even know what their boundaries are. It is very difficult to change something you don't know you have.

Setting boundaries depends on your previous experiences and upbringing. It might be easier for some people to establish boundaries than others because of such predispositions. It might take some learning, but if you are persistent, you will get it right.

First, you need to learn what you are about. What are your boundaries? You must acknowledge your feelings. Boundaries are only effective when you know what you are protecting, hence what you are shielding yourself from (Newland, 2008). Does someone's comment make you feel terrible? Do you feel drained when you are in their presence? This is a good place to start.

Learning about yourself helps you evaluate your actions and choices, and recognize how you feel. Most people have leaky boundaries in their relationships, and at some point they give up altogether. In such a relationship, you become so engrossed in your partner's life that you substitute your life for theirs. Relationships are about two unique individuals coming together to form a healthy unit.

Take some time to rethink your life. Reflect and check in with yourself until you are aware of the difference between your partner or the other party to this interaction, and yourself.

Second, how do you know when your boundaries are crossed? Once you are aware of your feelings, you know when you are hurt. That is the point your boundaries are breached. Ask yourself how was your boundary breached? Here are some examples.

Scenario 1:

"Your partner always promises to take you out and meet their friends and family, but it never happens."

Scenario 2:

"Someone in your life is always asking for money, promising to pay back but they never do."

Scenario 3:

"A close friend or family member keeps calling you in the middle of the night or messaging about their problems, but they don't seem interested in solving the problems themselves. Each time they call, you cannot fall asleep after the call."

Each time these events happen, something breaks inside you. You feel disappointed, unloved, cheated, unappreciated and so forth. You already know what matters to you, and how you feel when those feelings are not appreciated. Now, you know how your boundaries are breached.

Third, you focus on how to reset boundaries. You are in charge of your life, and to borrow a common phrase in many establishments, Management reserves the right of admission!

Why should you put up with someone who has made it clear they don't respect anything you say? Having realized the things that hurt you and how, the next step is to confront the problem. Address the person who keeps breaching your boundaries without a care.

Here are some examples on how to handle the scenarios above:

Scenario 1

Tell your partner why it bothers you that they haven't kept this promise. Tell them to stop making the promise altogether, and act on it once and get it out of the way.

Scenario 2

Remind them that since they have failed to honor their commitments, you will not lend them more money until they pay back what they owe.

Scenario 3

Tell your friend or family member that you understand their pain, but it is draining the life out of you. Ask them to seek professional help, and if possible, stop answering the calls.

By addressing these issues, you make the other person aware that they are hurting you, and they need to stop.

Fourth, you must learn how to ground your boundaries. Establishing boundaries is one thing, but maintaining them is not easy either. If you have weak boundaries, your partner will recognize this and can manipulate you into feeling guilty through backlash. However, the most important thing is that these boundaries are there for you.

You must respect your boundaries before you expect the same of someone else. Grounding your boundaries is more about awareness and strengthening your resolve. Meditation, deep breathing, chakra are some of the techniques you can use to enforce your boundaries.

While enforcing your boundaries, don't forget your emotions. They are valid. Trust in yourself. You are not wrong to set your boundaries. This is healthy, and everyone must respect each other's boundaries if you are to be happy together. You have individual boundaries and couple boundaries. Each of these boundaries are unique, and it is their independence that makes your relationship healthy.

Fifth, talk about your boundaries. Talk about it. Let your partner know you have boundaries and they have persistently crossed them, and you need them to stop. Fair warning, this might not always go well. If your partner retorts, argues back or lashes out at you for having boundaries, perhaps it is best you walk away and take care of yourself. It is clear that you are not a priority to them.

Backlash is usually one of the signs that someone does not acknowledge or respect your boundaries. Arguing with them about it is an acknowledgement of their disrespect, which opens room for unhealthy compromise. Boundaries are simple. If someone doesn't understand them, the best they can do is ask you to enlighten them about your boundaries and need thereof. This can help them understand you better, and why you need the boundaries.

Boundaries must come with consequences. People will always push your boundaries, at times just to see what happens. Decide on appropriate consequences and communicate them clearly. Setting consequences is the ultimate way of embracing your boundaries. Make this about you. After all, the purpose of boundaries is to honor your commitment to your inner peace, not to judge or satisfy another person's choices and actions.

Finally, take care of yourself. If the discussion about your boundaries did not go according to plan, don't spend your time worrying about it. Step outside, exercise, run along the beach, go for a walk or something. Do anything that will prevent you from spending a lot of your energy worrying about what transpired earlier.

3. Personal detachment

Narcissists will always project their flaws to you. They blame you for things that you have nothing to do with. They will undermine you and break your spirit. A good solution for this is to retreat and embrace a different approach so that you learn how to deal with their tirades.

Learn how to ignore their personal attacks. Don't take anything a narcissist says personally. When you do this, it is easier for you to handle the situation better. The last thing you want to do is pick up an argument with a narcissist because they will never listen to you. At best, let them know you don't agree with their position, and leave it at that.

Any encounter with a narcissist is most likely about them, and never about you. In order to identify and reject these attacks, you should understand your self-worth, believe in yourself, and shun any criticism that they might level against you.

4. Contextual evaluation

What is the situation at hand? Take time and learn the context before you respond to a narcissist. Some of their outbursts are not because they are narcissists but because of circumstances which eventually make them embrace the narcissistic personality.

A good example is when you are offered a promotion over your colleague who has a narcissistic personality, and was eyeing the position too. Working together might not be easy. Your colleague will easily resent you for no reason. They will highlight your mistakes and wonder how you got the job instead of them.

Even if your colleague is not usually a confronting person, they might develop a condescending attitude towards you. In any argument or disagreement, they will throw words like "so you think you are better than everyone else," to vent and air out their frustration. It is always wise to assess the context of these tirades so that you know what you are dealing with and why.

Tips for dealing with a narcissist

A lot of things might run through your mind when you encounter a narcissist. It is normal that you might be engulfed by the desire to flee the situation. While self-preservation is important, you should also have it at the back of your mind that narcissistic personality disorder is a real mental problem, and if possible, encourage the individual to seek medical attention.

Besides those who have NPD, there are individuals who portray narcissistic characteristics. It is quite helpful if you know how to handle such people. This helps in managing your expectations, and creating a safe environment for you to interact with them without their narcissistic tendencies taking over. Below are useful ideas that will help you manage the situation better:

- Acceptance

One of the first things you have to do is realize that this person is who they are. Accept them. There is no version of themselves that you can create in your mind that will change their behavior. Many victims of narcissistic abuse suffer because deep down they hold onto a fallacy that someday, the abuser might change their ways. The only thing that might happen is your life changing for the worst.

- Deny them attention

Narcissists are attention hogs. Since they thrive on attention, why not shut them out? These are people who will do anything to be recognized. The attention might be positive or negative, but they will still thrive off of it. If you give them all the attention they need, the only thing that happens is that you end up sacrificing what is important to you, to satisfy them. Attention seekers like these will never respect you. They never see you in the same way you see them.

- Establish boundaries

The trick is not just establishing boundaries, but creating very clear boundaries. Communicate. Talk to the other person about what you feel when they do something that exceeds your boundaries. Set consequences and make sure they are aware of what it will cost them the next time they cross your boundaries.

More importantly, hold them accountable for their actions. You have to be steadfast in your approach to dealing with narcissists. A narcissist will try to find the easiest way to get back control from you. While you set these boundaries, they might feel you are moving further away from them, which is infuriating. Instead, ensure you communicate the boundaries to them in a healthy way. Do it in a manner that does not feel like they are being attacked.

There are sacrifices you can make for people who are dear to you, like these ones. However, at the same time you must also be aware that some people might never change. If this is that kind of a person, then your personal safety and peace of mind comes first, and the best thing to do is to walk away. It does not matter if they are your parents, siblings or lovers; walking away might be the only way you stay alive.

- Retaliation

When you figure out how to handle a narcissist, do not assume they will take it kindly. Expect retaliation. Some mind tricks might be coming your way, so brace yourself for impact. One of the common responses to your boundaries is that they will also give you a list of their boundaries or demands. Be careful because what might seem like a counter offer to your boundaries might be a manipulation tactic.

It is common for a narcissist to state their terms in such a way that you feel guilty about your boundaries. They need you to go back to the drawing board and rethink your strategy. They can even make you feel like you are pushing them away. If you fall for this trick, you give up control of your life. Watch out for the sympathetic pleas, because in most cases, they are anything but sympathetic.

- Stand your ground

The last thing you can expect from a narcissist is that they will admit they made a mistake, or take responsibility for hurting you. Instead of owning up to it, it is easier for them to make you bear the responsibility for their actions. This is why you must always stand your ground. Be strong in your resolve because you know what is right. Do not give in to the manipulation. Theirs is an inflated ego that you can never truly please. Accepting the blame will only create more trouble for you in the future.

- No promises

You might have learned this about your partner already, their promises never materialize. You cannot keep up that unhealthy cycle. Instead of worrying about what happens next, insist on immediate action. If they promise you something, make sure they do it right away. Hold them accountable for it and insist on action.

The reason why you need to do this is because most of the time, promises from narcissists are nothing but a means to an end. Whenever they make a promise, there is something they want from you. Once they have it, the promises become a distant memory.

The Narcissist's False Self And True Self

Not all relationships are toxic and imbalanced, and even so, a majority of relationships, even platonic or work-related ones, will develop patterns. Patterns are evident in our daily life activities: the pattern of your workday, the pattern when you come home, the routine with your spouse or partner about who cooks and who cleans after supper, or the routine or pattern of when you go to sleep and your nighttime rituals.

All patterns begin somewhere and develop or change over time, and in any relationship, you have in your life, a lot of patterns will change while many stay the same. If you tend to date men or women who have certain tendencies or attributes, in this case, NPD, then you will already be comfortable with these patterns, and perhaps, not realize that you are repeating the same patterns over and over again by being drawn to similar types of people.

Patterns are the life grooves that get worn into our consciousness and mental state. They are the basis of how we think, react, feel, and treat others and ourselves. Patterns, like bad habits, can be broken and will only require that you acknowledge what the patterns are in the first place so that you know what needs to change.

As with any relationship, typical narcissistic relationships will follow a general pattern that causes the partners involved to exist in a repetitive cycle. Otherwise, the pattern is the general rule of thumb for how the narcissist will operate in every relationship. The usual pattern has three stages, including idealizing the partner, devaluing them, and finally discarding them. It is an emotional rollercoaster, and it can repeat itself, depending on how many times you are willing to go on this ride without facing the truth of what is going on.

Let's explore the stages so that you figure out what stage you might currently be in with your partner, or if you can recognize a common theme in your relationship from these patterns.

Idealize

In the first stages of the romantic partnership, a narcissistic person will create a reality with their partner that involves a feeling of infatuation and otherworldliness, almost as if it was destiny that the two of you came together. The sensation is of true love and a beautiful and inspiring courtship coming into being. Some people have described this part of the stage as intoxicating or like being on a drug and the high lasts for weeks, months, and occasionally longer than that.

It is not abnormal to feel the love high in the beginning stages of any relationship, and it is greatly common for couples to inspire this feeling in each other as they get closer and form the love bond. In the case of the narcissistic relationship, the following stages offer a broader explanation of how it is different than other love relationships in their blossoming stage.

People who have reported being in narcissistic relationships have described the "idealize" stage like finding a soulmate and are on a cloud of beautiful life possibilities with their partner. The sensation is that you will never fall apart and that you are meant to be together. This connection is offered greatly by the narcissist who will "drug" their partner with loving words, dedications, praise, courting rituals, intense sexual relations, regular vacations or trips, promises of creating a future life together, and the admonishment of being the most important and special person they have ever met.

It sounds amazing, doesn't it? And who wouldn't want to have such a whirlwind romance right from the get-go? Isn't that what every romantic comedy is selling to you? The "love bomb" phase of the relationship feels like a dream come true, and the reality is that anyone who experienced something like this would probably have a hard time being skeptical, especially when they are being promised the world and that love will last forever.

The next stage creates the platform for understanding the true nature of the narcissistic relationship after the "honeymoon" phase has worn out their ability to gain "narcissistic supply."

Devalue

As the relationship enters a more realistic and comfortable rhythm, the intensity may not be as extreme, and some aspects of the connection may start to wane or grown faded. There are moments of disagreement and possible attempts to confront the narcissist about their attitude or behavior, with a reaction that is not what you might expect from someone who is so deeply in love with you, as they demonstrated before.

The large, red flags on the tropical paradise, love island you created together start to paint another picture of reality. It happens slowly and subtly and can sometimes even feel stealthy, cunning, and deceptive. The objective of the narcissist is to devalue their partner in covert ways to attain a level of emotional superiority, in effect, causing their partner to establish an urge or desire to rekindle the level of affection that they had experienced in the first stages of becoming acquainted with each other.

The narcissist quietly bullies while their partner, or the victim of narcissistic abuse, works tirelessly to bring the sensuality and love back into the courtship by falling for the game and asking the narcissist what they can do to change or "fix it."

In a lot of situations, a person might see these red flags and not feel attached to the narcissist, choosing instead to let the relationship naturally dissolve into the final stage (discarding). However, in many cases, the partner of the narcissist will want to remind themselves of how magical the opening of the affair was and that it must be true love, and therefore, worth seeking out solutions to whatever issues are arising.

The patterns will continue in the "devaluing" stage, as the narcissist will not want to comply with any kind of growth and will create emotional and mental (occasionally physical) abuse in the form of gaslighting, putting down their partner with verbal comments, avoiding or withdrawing emotional or physical intimacy as a form of punishment, disappearing for periods of time without word, withholding seduction or affection, and blaming their partner for anything that might be an issue with them (projecting).

This stage can continue for a while, but eventually, if the partner of the narcissist is not complying with their demands, needs, and expectations, then they will be discarded and cast off.

Discard

If the partner of the narcissist cannot provide them with adequate narcissistic supply, then they will be discarded without emotion or need for debate. If the partner asks for a kind of compromise, honesty, relationship counseling, healthy boundaries, or mutual exchange, then the narcissist will likely determine that they are no longer with the "perfect partner." What they want is someone who can always feed their ego without the demand for anything else in return, and so, if you are not able to meet these demands, you are no longer a viable partner for the narcissist.

Keep in mind, as you read this that it is totally and completely normal and healthy to ask for reciprocity, balance, comradery, communication, and compromise in your relationships. These qualities and attributes, however, are not commonly practiced by the narcissist and so you will be throwing bricks at a brick wall for no good reason if you ask them to compromise or see your side of things.

In a codependent partnership or a situation between a narcissist and an empath, the relationship can be a lifelong pattern(idealize, devalue, discard - over and over again) that will never fully reach a full discarding of the relationship. However, the act of discarding can occur as a result of not meeting the narcissist's needs, and it will be an emotional discarding and punishment that can only be rectified by the partner of the narcissist succumbing to the emotional needs and demands of the narcissist's ego.

Either way, the discarding stage can feel like a huge shock to the victim or target of narcissistic abuse, because it began with such passion, love, and admiration. How can such a loving and amiable person become so different and not even care about your special bond? The answer is that they never truly cared and they were simply looking for someone to feed their ego and offer them narcissistic supply. If you can't meet that demand, then you're out.

Unfortunately, this can happen all of the time, especially if you don't know what patterns or flags to observe when you are getting involved with someone. The key is identifying the patterns in the devaluing stage so that you don't end up shocked, confused, and alone with a stack of insecurities and neuroses about yourself that you were convinced of having by your narcissistic partner.

The effects of this pattern over time can be exhausting and detrimental to you. If you have already engaged in this type of pattern before and you keep going through it with certain patterns, stop blaming yourself for the relationship ending after such a whirlwind start. Odds are, it's not your fault and whatever your narcissistic partner told you about yourself is not true.

Chapter 4 Narcissistic Personality Disorder

hew, there were a lot of symptoms to cover! But nevertheless, we think that it's extremely important to get know each and every one of them, and most importantly, to see how they are manifested in the real world. "Real world? you might ask, "but you've talked so much about some fictional characters and literature! What's real in that?". The thing is, although literature isn't necessarily correct in the literal sense, some characters and situations described in good literature seem as truthful as the chair you're sitting on.

But now that we're finished, we will pass on to other topics that will take everything we've said so far and put it into a wider context. Already, we have mentioned some wide-scale consequences of narcissism. Wars, corrupt ideologies, murders, these things can all happen as a result of untamed and uncontrolled narcissistic traits.

Terrorism

Terrorism is the modern day's plague. It can take many forms, but, of course, the most shocking and appalling ones get the most media coverage. And these cases of terrorism are linked with narcissism. And this is not a coincidence. In big media coverage and fame, narcissistic terrorists seek and find the admiration they need. Or, as Brad Bushman has put it "As ego deflates, the aggression inflates."- It is not much different with admiration. The more they long for excessive admiration, the more extreme their methods become.

We'll analyze only a few cases, starting from the Columbine School Shooting.

The two perpetrators of that horrible misdeed, Eric Harris and Dylan Klebold, were only teenagers at the time. They murdered 12 and injured 21 people, most of them were children, Eric and Dylan's former classmates. One, of course, has to ask: "Why?" and unfortunately, there isn't a simple answer. For instance, various researchers concluded that Dylan Klebold exhibited major signs of depression- "Dylan wanted to die and didn't care if others died as well."

But Eric Harris' story is different. Besides being a psychopath, Eric Harris most probably had reached an almost delusional level of grandiosity and superiority complex. By killing and injuring countless persons he wanted to show his power and might to the world. Unlike Dylan, he "...wanted to kill others and didn't care if he died in the process." It's obvious that in Eric, we have the deadly combination of psychopathic and narcissistic traits. Also, he considered himself as the mastermind of their deadly plan and regarded this "feat" as his work of art. So Klebold simply wanted to end his life, while Harris clearly wanted to show his greatness to the world. His delusions where so overwhelmingly vivid that he would rather lose his life than let them pale in the light of reality.

Harris' private journal is of great importance for our conclusions. In his journal, he mostly talks about his "right" to do anything he wants, and that anyone who dares to even try and take this "right" away from him will be annihilated. For instance, speaking about a minor theft he committed previously, Harris writes about this little incident and says that if he wants to take something, he has an absolute entitlement to that object. Finally, it is alleged that shooting was Harris' idea in the first place. However, this statement is often contested, but one thing is clear- Harris was probably much more enthusiastic about the shooting than Klebold, and it is not impossible that he coaxed Klebold into committing this horrible crime.

Let's analyze another case, probably the worst shooting of all times- Breivik's attacks in Norway. Being a lone wolf attacker, Anders Breivik is an even better example of how terrorism and narcissism are inextricably linked. Breivik first detonated a car bomb in Oslo's center. Oslo is the capital city, so all eyes were turned towards the city's center. And this was a perfect diversion. Shortly after the detonation; Anders Breivik, armed to the teeth headed for the island where the youth division of Norway's Labor party camped. As soon as he disembarked from the boat, he started shooting everywhere. Epilogue: 69 teenagers murdered, 110 injured, 55 seriously wounded. Add the casualties of the car bomb that exploded earlier to that- 8 people died, while 209 were injured. If you do the math, you will see that Breivik affected lives; 396 teens. This is why it's so important to talk about this disorder. If everyone knew just a bit more about the signs and symptoms of the disorder, men like Breivik could be stopped before they commit their horrible crimes. But let's get back to our current topic.

Although it looks as if Breivik's main motives were purely political, this most surely isn't the case. Or even if political motives played a role, it was a minor and minuscule one. The chief thing is that Breivik, by adopting extreme far-right views, got the opportunity to regard himself as a "warrior", or "saver", someone who will singlehandedly stop the Islamization of Europe. Needless to say, this kind of thinking doesn't come without extreme fantasies of grandeur. Breivik thought that Europe is no good with the current politics, and he wanted to be seen as a savior, almost as a messiah, someone who would save the country from the ongoing scourge. He could be described as a Nazi. He also openly praised the Srebrenica massacre, as in this little Bosnian town, some 8 thousand Muslims were massacred by the Republic of Srpska army. This all happened prior to the massacre Breivik himself committed. Let's leave the rest to the expert, Brad Busman: "The gunman was diagnosed with narcissistic personality disorder, along with several other mental disorders. Narcissistic tendencies can also be seen in his manifesto, where he rewrites his life history by fabricating his supposed accomplishments (e.g., being part of one of the toughest gangs, being a prominent graffiti artist with works all over the city, being a high-ranking Freemason), and describes himself as a revolutionary leader, an international political leader, and a patriot with a large number of followers."

As was the case with Sergey Nechayev, political attitudes and opinions were only a charade for deep, relentless egocentrism. This is at the same time why we mentioned Nechayev's story in the first place- to show how narcissists exist through centuries and influence history.

We'll give a short list of other shootings that shook the world:

1. At Simon's Rock College of Bard, MA, in 1992. The gunman took the lives of two while wounding 4 people. A psychiatrist concluded that the attacker suffered from narcissistic personality disorder, and had an inflated image of himself.

2. In 1997, a massacre happened at one Mississippi high school, where 1 was killed and 7 more injured. Here, there was no question - three psychologists, independent from one another, concluded that the attacker suffered from NPD.

3. At Case Western University, Ohio, in 2003, the attacker killed one and seriously wounded two students, after which he was overpowered by a SWAT team. A psychologist, who spoke with the

gunman on numerous occasions which totaled to 11 hours of observation, concluded that the Case Western University attacker had narcissistic personality disorder.

4. At Arapahoe High School in Colorado, in 2013, one student was killed, although it could have been much worse as the perpetrator brought 125 rounds of ammunition, a shotgun, and few Molotov cocktails. Fortunately, he didn't succeed in setting fire to the school. A school psychologist believed that the attacker had NPD.

The relationship between narcissism and violence

Over the years, a lot of authors supported the thesis that low self-esteem leads to violence. It's obvious that with this stance, we're not going to get anywhere with our explanations of narcissistic violence. A lot of more recent studies showed that narcissism is indeed linked with violence and aggressive behavior, and this link is far from being weak. The newest research suggests that individuals with inflated egos are more likely to exhibit aggressive behavior towards others. More specifically; it is the instability of their inflated self-concept that leads them towards committing such atrocious crimes. This is sometimes called threatened egotism. Narcissists are the most dangerous when their fantasies and unrealistic representations are brought to question. To defend these fantasies, some people resort to extreme measures. Eric Harris, whose personality we've tried to describe as concisely as possible, for sure acted in the goal of protecting his egotism. Is there a better way to affirm one's might, one's "lust for life" than by taking those same characteristics from others.

Here we come to an important point. The more threatened the ego, the more likely is a person to act aggressively. And this statement has important consequences when deciding how to deal with narcissists.

Let's say that you realized that your dear friend is actually a covert narcissist. It's obvious that he's fond of you, and up until now, you've met on a regular basis. There are few alternatives you can choose to try and deal with this problem. Of course, upon realizing the true nature of your friend, you will most likely either try to help him or break all contacts. Both alternatives are pretty dangerous. If you opt for the first one, you will be faced with an almost insurmountable hurdle. By being direct and honest, you will most likely cause a brusque and harsh response. In other words, you'll threaten the egotism of your friend and bring yourself to an inconvenient position, open confrontation, verbal abuse, or even physical violence are just some of the things that come to mind.

On the other hand, you might opt to break all contacts altogether. This alternative is not much different from the first one, at least when it comes to your friend's response. Like any human being, your friend would be hurt and would suffer emotionally. But, unlike other, normal human beings, your friend will project all the pain, everything that goes on in his mind onto you. His ego being shaken by the rejection, he'll seek to foster it by hurting you personally. By doing this, he will affirm that the problem isn't within him, but within you. And this kind of response should always be expected. Because, if your narcissistic friend didn't begin to insult and attack you, what is left for him to do? To question himself? and finally destroy the remainders of his shaken ego? Never.

As already mentioned, some narcissists would rather die than change their overinflated self-images. Eric Harris stands as a reminder of this bitter fact. Breivik, on the other hand, was different. He didn't kill himself after his deadly spree has ended. He continues to live, probably without a trace of repentance and penitence. Breivik is, in a way, the true narcissist. He wanted to live and see the consequences of his actions.

Don't think that we're just speculating here. There are experiments, done by an expert in this field (the aforementioned Bushman), that show just how dangerous narcissists are. In his experiment, Bushman first caused anger in his subjects. After doing this, he gave them the opportunity to express their anger- either towards an innocent person or towards a person who insulted them. As expected, narcissists were most likely to express their anger, and they were the most aggressive towards the person who caused their anger. Have this in mind the next time you're dealing with a narcissist. Most importantly, the seriousness of the insult was in relation to the intensity of the wrath. So, our statement - The more threatened the ego, the more likely is a person to act aggressively- has been experimentally proved.

Narcissistic abuse syndrome

Narcissistic abuse is a thing. It happens, and it has serious consequences for the well-being of its victims. This syndrome is relatively unknown, especially when compared to other stress disorders, like Posttraumatic Stress Disorder, that has been in the center of attention since the first Vietnam War veterans returned to the USA. And this is why we want to describe and the narcissistic abuse syndrome (NAS). Note that there are several slightly different terminological solutions- we refer to the disorder as narcissistic abuse syndrome, but it is often referred to as narcissistic victim syndrome, or even narcissistic victim abuse syndrome. These little differences aren't that important. What is important is the problem itself.

This syndrome refers to any kind of abuse committed by a narcissist. It mostly concerns emotional abuse but isn't confined to this particular type. There are many subtypes of this syndrome, of which parental narcissistic abuse syndrome is the most well-known one. In this case, the parent becomes excessively controlling and autocratic. We all know that type of parent that has already planned the next 20 years of a 2-year-old child. They overburden their children with innumerable obligations, like sports, instrument playing, school-related activities, etc. This might not be that big of a problem, only if narcissistic parents weren't so aggressive when their child fails. Just imagine being a child who is constantly dragged from one activity to the other. After your swimming class, you rush to piano lessons. And, as if this wasn't enough of a drag, your parent(s) gets extremely angry at you when you aren't the best one in your group.

The situation is a bit different with adult-to-adult relationships. Besides our main antagonist, narcissist, another type of individuals steps into the game- dependent persons.

By finding a dependent person, a narcissist gets all the admiration he needs. On the other hand, the dependent person finally finds someone who will take control. By choosing a narcissistic individual, not only will they find someone who will control them, but also someone who will enjoy doing this. Needless to say, these relationships rarely have a happy ending. It is much more likely that it ends up in a cycle of abuse, where the dependent person formed a bond so strong that abuse isn't seen as a problem. They will endure anything in order to retain their traumatic bond.

A little disclaimer; Narcissistic abuse syndrome is something that has only recently begun to be researched. So there still is a lot to be learned about this syndrome, from a scientific point of view. We won't give lists of symptoms or anything like that, as there still isn't a list of symptoms that has been scientifically validated. Rather, we will only mention the most important signs of narcissistic abuse syndrome.

Probably the most important thing about NAS is the fact that victims rarely mention their real cause of problems in therapy. They will often come to therapy and complain about something that doesn't have even the remotest connection to the abuser. They will come and say: "I feel a bit depressed lately.", or "My husband told me that I need to get some help." They will usually blame some irrelevant factors. But, little by little, a good therapist will begin to know what he's dealing with.

Second thing, if the therapist tries to confront the victim with the real cause of problems, even if his confrontation is only a mild and careful one, he will encounter strong resistance. People with narcissistic abuse syndrome will seldom, if ever admit that the person whom they idolize is bad. They may something like: "Yes, my husband is sometimes a very nervous and anxious person. But even when he does bad things, I know that he didn't really want to do them. He's not that sort of person". In statements like these, there is a lot to be analyzed. For example, you probably noted how the victim said "nervous" and "anxious". These are classical euphemisms for aggressive and abusing behavior. Of course, it's much easier to say that someone is nervous than saying that he is aggressive, especially when we idolize that person. Secondly, in statements like this last one, we can see how the victim, while admitting that their abuser can be bad, don't believe that this badness is his inherent characteristic. The bad behavior is perceived as something that just "doesn't go with his personality." However, there must be someone to blame. And it is not rare to see the victim of narcissistic abuse blaming herself for her husband's misdeeds.

Furthermore, victims are often filled with feelings of shame and guilt. They suffer, but they don't know why. As mentioned, there must be someone to blame, and if the victim blames herself, what are the most logical emotions to ensue- of course, shame, guilt, low self-esteem, etc. This only makes the situation even worse, as the person lacks the power of will to face her present and future struggles. What do we mean by "present and future struggles"? Well, for starters, we supposed that a vast majority of people who suffer from narcissistic abuse syndrome aren't aware of the real cause of their troubles, at least in the initial period. This initial period of the disorder can be of lesser intensity when compared to the latter phases of the disorder. By "present struggles", we wanted to say that the victim first has to know the real truth. That is the first and sometimes the most important hurdle on the way towards recuperation.

Future struggles come when the person finally becomes aware, and when idolization of the abuser begins to pale. This is probably the most challenging phase, as the person has to face the fact that she devoted years of her life to the man who actually despises her and has continually hurt her over the years. Memories of past traumas that have been repressed up until now all come to the surface. The victim finds herself overburdened by vivid, relentless visions of traumatic events. These memories also haunt their dreams. Victims' lives become completely absorbed by the past. Everything they do, every little thing they own, everything points to their wound that looks as if it will never heal. Despair, sulk, depression slowly enter the victims' lives. Finally, people who suffer from narcissistic abuse syndrome may have problems with forming new interpersonal relations. After all, they have been hurt so bad, it is reasonable to be suspicious and on alarm every time a new person appears. So, not only does the victim suffer emotionally, but she is also unable to find support in others.

There are other peripheral symptoms. Depressive people might have some cognitive difficulties- problems with attention, short and long-term memory. Work performance might decrease severely. In short, the whole life, every little aspect is influenced by the abuse they endured. Luckily, this is not something that stays for good. When treated, victims of NAS get back to their usual levels of performance, which is why it's very important to appropriately treat this disorder.

NAS is quite similar to PTSD. For example, we've mentioned that people with NAS have nightmares and cognitive deficits, which is also the case with people who have PTSD. Moreover; people with PTSD avoid situations that have some connection to the traumatic event. For example, a soldier who was severely traumatized during the war may avoid seeing his fellow veterans. He may avoid movies with war-thematic. Similarly; the individual with NAS may avoid any situation that will remind her of her abuser. Mutual friends, places they have visited together, the house they lived together, even their kids, all this might remind her of her abuser.

There are other similarities. Recurring thoughts, memories about the initial trauma happen in both disorders. Vivid, almost life-like "flashbacks" of the traumatic event, although one of the major symptoms of PTSD might as well appear in NAS. Especially in cases when the person is surrounded with objects that remind her of her abuser, these flashbacks are highly likely. And they feel like going through hell all over again. Also, people with PTSD and NAS experience extreme sensitivity and reactivity to unexpected, sudden stimuli. This shows how defensive they become. They are so traumatized they always watch out for threats. It's obvious that this hypervigilance is something extremely exhausting. Imagine being 24/7 on the alarm; always being afraid of some unexpected disaster. You don't sleep, eat, or smile. Nothing stays the same. Hell on Earth.

Let's see how Patrick Carnes, counselor, and famous best-selling writer, systematized traumatic response. He discerned 8 major groups of symptoms:

1. Reaction- we've mentioned some of these symptoms. They are usually seen in PTSD when people avoid situations that might remind them of their trauma. Recurrent memories, thoughts, and images of the trauma itself also fall within this group.

2. Arousal- this is an obscure part of trauma, and rarely debated. We could say that this is a "pleasurable" part of trauma. In other words, victims of narcissistic abuse, although severely traumatized, sometimes experience positive emotions in relation to their abuser, which, of course, makes the situation even more confusing for them.

3. Blocking- cognitive problems, depression, indifference, lack of motivation, and numbing. These and other symptoms represent a way to adapt to the horrible consequences of the abuse. It is sometimes much better to completely "turn off", and become numb than to continuously think about the trauma. So, once again, the term maladaptation is pertinent.

4. Splitting- when a person goes through extreme abuse and trauma (such happens during a war), the reality can just become too much. It becomes impossible to block unwanted thoughts entering the mind, even with depression and numbing. So a person has to resort to another means- making up her own fantasy world. It slowly becomes obvious

that the real, harsh reality is completely dissociated from the fantasy world, there are no overlaps.

5. Abstinence- this is a somewhat more constructive way of dealing with abuse. It is not unusual to see the victim become completely immersed in her work. When this happens, victim closely resembles individuals with obsessive-compulsive personality disorder. For example, they begin hoarding money, without any special goal or intention. The victim exerts herself and works long hours. Social functioning may suffer as a result. The victim just doesn't have enough time to hang out with other people, and even if she did, she feels awkward in the company of others and isn't sure how to behave around other people.

6. Shame- there was already much talk on shame and guilt. Simply put; when victims reflect on the years of their life that passed in utter suffering, they cannot shake off the impression that they were extremely stupid, submissive, or even that they are to blame for the unfortunate events that happened.

7. Trauma repetition- it is not unusual to see the victim returning to her abuser. This is the so-called vicious cycle of abuse. As mentioned before, the relationship between the abuser and his victim is almost always an ambiguous one. Yes, there is a lot of bad stuff

going on, but sometimes, the victim may feel some positive emotions in relation to her abuser. And her dependency, her belief that the abuser "finally changed" and "got back to his senses" is what gets her to forget everything bad that happened. And we all know what happens after.

8. Trauma bonds- it is not unusual to see the victim still cherishing some positive emotions towards her abuser. For example, William Faulkner, although a good writer, was a very difficult man. He drank profusely and was particularly aggressive at times. His lover, Meta Wilde, often had to endure Faulkner's fits of rage. But she never left him, always returning even after severe physical abuse she suffered.

Chapter 5 Narcissistic Manipulation Tactics

The Cycle of Abuse

The key to understanding narcissistic abuse is to understand what the narcissist is looking for in a relationship. Narcissists are always looking for someone to admire them, someone to reinforce the ideal self they've created. This feeling of being admired and praised is called "narcissistic supply," and everything the narcissist does is done for the purpose of either maintaining one source of narcissistic supply or cultivating a new source.

In parent-to-child narcissistic relationships, the narcissistic parent treats the child as a permanent source of narcissistic supply and does everything possible to prevent the child from ever becoming an independent person through guilt-tripping, belittling, and other abusive behaviors.

In adult-to-adult narcissistic relationships, the narcissist comes on strong in the early stages with an idealized and ultimately imaginary version of his real personality. The ideal self isn't real, so the narcissist won't be able to keep up the façade. The true self slips out, and the narcissist does something abusive and damaging. When the mask is restored, the victim is once again shown the idealized self. This emotional roller coaster can result in something called "trauma bonding," where the victim actually gets emotionally closer to the abuser as a result of the abuse. Even though the victim may want to believe that the idealized version of the narcissist is real, and the abusive behavior is the exception, the truth is the exact opposite.

In the end, the narcissist will seek out a new source of narcissistic supply, discarding the old relationship as if it never meant anything. In some cases, the narcissist will hover in the background rather than completely disappearing. By going away and then coming back, the narcissist can keep the victim from ever moving on and ensure his own access to the narcissistic supply.

The Five Stages of Abuse

The cycle of abuse can be divided into five stages, marked by different types of abusive behavior—some of which will not appear abusive at first. The first stage is gaining trust, in which the abuser idealizes the victim and acts loving, kind, and sweet. In cases of narcissistic abuse, this is when the narcissist will present only the false or idealized self.

The second stage is over-involvement, in which the abuser works his way into every little detail of the victim's life. Healthy boundaries are slowly eroded until the victim can no longer tell what a boundary violation is and what is not.

The third stage is rulemaking, in which the abuser sets the terms of the relationship through jealous and controlling behavior. This is presented by the abuser as an expression of their love for the victim, but the level of jealousy and micromanaging extends far beyond normal relationship insecurity.

The fourth stage deals with control, in which the abuser gains power over the victim through all kinds of abuse and manipulation. Most of the obviously abusive behaviors don't occur until this stage when the victim already has a diminished ability to recognize and respond to what is happening.

The fifth stage is trauma bonding, where the abuser once again presents the ideal self for a time to draw the victim closer again.

Methods of Control

Once you understand that the abuser's manipulative and controlling behaviors are part of a pattern, it should be easier to recognize specific abusive behaviors for what they are. The narcissistic abuser's methods of control include:

- Superficial charm

- Love bombing

- Nagging

- Ignoring

- Punishment

- Guilt Tripping

- Emotional Blackmail

- Isolation

- Mind Games

- Gaslighting

- Blaming the Victim

Superficial Charm

"Superficial charm" is the narcissist's version of courtship behavior. The narcissist is slick and likable, but there is nothing behind it because the charming behavior is only an expression of the false self the narcissist has created. Narcissistic parents may use superficial charm when interacting with anyone outside the household, such as teachers or social workers. In a dating relationship, the narcissist uses superficial charm to gain the victim's trust.

Narcissists in the early stages of a relationship may appear to be unusually romantic, attentive, and complimentary. They may seem to idealize you or to have a lot in common with you—perhaps too much to be completely believable. One tactic of psychological control is "ingratiation," in which the abuser gains your trust by deliberately mirroring your likes and dislikes.

In reality, these behaviors are all part of the act. It isn't easy to tell the difference between superficial charm and genuine goodwill, but if your instincts are telling you that something is off, then you should slow down and pay close attention to other red flags such as "love bombing."

Love Bombing

The term "love bombing" originally referred to as a recruitment tactic used by some cult groups. Potential members of the cult would be drawn in through intense displays of positive attention and affection combined with strong pressure to join the group. Later on, mental health counselors started to use the term to describe a similar tactic often used by narcissistic abusers.

To a lonely person looking for love and affection, a sudden and over-the-top display of love can be like a drug. It feels so good that you just want more. The narcissist knows this and uses the "love bomb" to draw the victim in. The intense positive attention is combined with pressure to commit quickly, escalating the relationship to a higher level much faster than most people would usually be comfortable with.

The combination of affection and pressure creates a sense of anxiety, as the victim doesn't want to miss out on the chance at "true love" by resisting the narcissist's wishes. The pressure to commit is also a test, in which the narcissist is trying to find out whether the target will set a firm boundary or not. When the victim gives in to the pressure and agrees to a commitment, the narcissist is already in the second stage of abuse—the stage of over-involvement.

Of course, it can be hard to tell whether someone is love bombing you or genuinely falling in love with you. The main difference is consistency. Love bombing is shallow and is always followed by devaluation. From being idealized, you become the object of contempt and derision. Real love isn't like that, but the only certain way to tell the difference between the two is to wait and see. That's why it's so important not to get carried away and escalate the relationship too quickly—especially if you're feeling pressured.

Nagging

Superficial charm and love bombing are both types of positive reinforcement, in which you are rewarded with positive attention for doing what the abuser wants you to do. Nagging is a type of negative reinforcement in which you are pressured to do what the abuser wants you to do.

Nagging isn't always abusive. Parents nag children to clean up their rooms, and children nag parents for candy or screen time. As annoying as that can be, it doesn't constitute abuse. Abusive nagging happens when you try to set a healthy boundary, and the abuser wears your boundary down with repeated requests. Like many other kinds of subtle manipulation, nagging always has plausible deniability. If you call out the narcissist for pushing your boundaries, she can always claim that she was "only asking" and accuse you of being oversensitive.

In a healthy relationship, some decisions are shared equally between both parties, and some decisions are yours alone. You may be the victim of abusive nagging if the other person is always pressuring you to agree to their wishes on shared decisions or to let them influence decisions that should be yours to make. Nagging is a common tactic in narcissistic parenting but is also used by narcissists in other types of relationships.

Ignoring

Ignoring or shunning is another type of negative reinforcement. This includes "the silent treatment," withholding affection, and so on. It can be as overt as simply refusing to speak to you or acknowledge your presence, or as covert as a vague but persistent atmosphere of emotional coldness and rejection.

Ignoring goes hand in hand with love bombing even though the two may seem to be opposites. First, the abuser gives you the addictive drug of intense affection and admiration—then, she cuts it off completely if you don't do what she wants. Desperate to get the feelings back, you quickly cave in under pressure—and the abuser gains more control.

Some narcissists will alternate positive reinforcement and negative reinforcement just to leave you off-balance and emotionally dependent. This tactic is known as intermittent reinforcement. Through acting cold and dismissive one moment and extremely sweet the next, the abuser creates a situation where the victim is constantly chasing after them and trying to win their approval and affection back.

When the abuser starts being sweet again after ignoring or being cold to you, the relief can be so intense that you actually crave their affection even more than before. This is one example of trauma bonding, where the abuse brings you closer to the abuser in a profoundly toxic way.

Punishment

Ignoring and nagging can both used as types of punishment, along with other behaviors such as yelling, swearing at you, or dramatic emotional displays. By flipping out and making a huge scene when you don't do what he wants, the abuser makes you reluctant to go against his wishes in the future.

One of the most dramatic and frightening types of punishment is "narcissistic rage," where the narcissist responds with total fury to even the slightest hint of criticism. The narcissist may lash out with intentionally vicious personal attacks, escalating in some cases to property destruction or physical violence.

Narcissistic rage has two sides to it. On the one hand, the narcissist's self-image is a fragile veneer covering a much more profound self-loathing. Any criticism destroys the illusion, forcing the narcissist to confront the intolerably painful reality. To this extent, the rage is real.

On the other hand, the narcissist uses her rage to intimidate and manipulate the victim, by creating such a horrible scene that the victim will feel very reluctant ever to criticize the narcissist again. From this perspective, narcissistic rage is just a tactic of manipulation and control.

Sobbing, playing the victim, and threats of self-harm can also be used as forms of punishment. It can be hard to tell whether a person is intentionally trying to punish you or is simply feeling emotional. As always, the key is to see if there is an ongoing pattern. If there is a heavy price tag whenever you fail to do what the other person wants, then it's probably safest to assume they're doing it intentionally.

Guilt Tripping

The guilt trip is one type of punishment behavior. This behavior is especially common when dealing with a narcissistic parent, but it can also be found in other relationships.

The person who is trying to guilt-trip you accuses you of not really loving them, not caring about their problems, or of having done something to harm them in the past. Once they can see that you are feeling guilty, they give you the chance to be absolved of your guilt, but only if you do what they want. For instance, a narcissistic parent may guilt trip you into spending time with them instead of a friend, which also has the effect of isolating you.

Guilt-tripping only works on a person who cares about being loving and kind. It's painful to be told that you aren't a good person, so you're strongly motivated to do whatever it takes to avoid that. Unfortunately, this makes you vulnerable to manipulation.

Of course, if you were really such a terrible and uncaring person, then no one could make you feel guilty in the first place because you just wouldn't care. If someone wants you to feel like a bad person, you should ask yourself what they want from you. If it's something you wouldn't normally do, then they may simply be trying to use your guilt to get past your healthy boundaries and gain control over your decisions.

Emotional Blackmail Tactics

There are four different types of emotional blackmail tactics, as identified by the therapists Forward and Frazier in their study of the topic.

The first type is the threat of punishment, which includes several of the other tactics discussed in this chapter. For example, "Have sex with me, or I'll give you the silent treatment for the next three days," or "Add my name to your bank account, or I'll call off our engagement." The threat of punishment doesn't have to be explicitly stated; it can just as easily be implied.

The second type of emotional blackmail is the threat of self-harm. This is also a type of guilt trip because the obvious implication is that you are responsible for what happens next. "If you break up with me, I'll kill myself" is the clearest example of this tactic.

The third type of emotional blackmail is based on a display of self-pity. This is another type of guilt trip, in which the abuser does something nice for you but makes a big deal about the huge sacrifice they're making. For example, "I cooked you your favorite dinner even though I have a terrible headache." The idea is to put you in their debt so they can have more leverage over you.

The fourth type of emotional blackmail is to imply that you'll get a reward of some kind if you do whatever the other person wants you to do. This is different from a straightforward exchange of favors because it's used to pressure you into doing something you don't really want to do. In one way or another, it doesn't feel like an equal exchange.

Emotional blackmail tactics can be used for different purposes. Sometimes, they are used to get you to do something little that you might easily have agreed to anyway. Sometimes, they are used to get you to agree to something you're uncomfortable with, but that is still fairly minor in the big scheme of things. Sometimes, they are used to influence your life decisions, such as where to live or whether to go to school. In the most extreme scenario, emotional blackmail can even be used to convince you to participate in criminal behavior.

Isolation Tactics

The narcissistic abuser may use any of these manipulation and control tactics to isolate you from the other people in your life. For example, if you make plans to see a friend for coffee, a narcissistic partner may nag you to change your plans, or give you the silent treatment when you get home or accuse you of not wanting to spend any time with him. He may use emotional blackmail, saying, "Of course I don't mind if you go out with your friends, all I want is for you to be happy. It's just that I've been feeling so depressed."

Whatever specific tactic the narcissist uses, the end result is the same—you find it so difficult to make plans with your friends that you gradually stop doing so, and the narcissist increasingly becomes your only source of emotional support. This not only makes it less likely that you will decide to leave, but it also feeds into the narcissist's own need to be the center of your world.

Mind Games

Abusers often play mind games to keep their victims disoriented and passive. For example, an abuser may set you up to fail by giving you a task without the time or resources needed to complete it successfully. If you accomplish something you're proud of, the abuser may minimize it or refuse to acknowledge it. The abuser may repeatedly remind you of past failures or mistakes, or he may "shift the goalposts" so you're always trying to catch up with an ever-changing set of expectations. He may use a one-sided story about your relationship as a type of propaganda, leading you to accept a distorted view of past events. This is also a type of brainwashing, where the abuser seeks to alter your ability to process reality and form your own opinions about it.

Gaslighting

If you bring up issues in the relationship or things that have hurt your feelings, the abuser may try to convince you that you are simply irrational and that your concerns have no validity. This is known as "gaslighting," the process of making someone doubt their own experiences and memories so they will not question or attempt to resist abuse.

For example, a narcissist who's cheating on you may try to convince you that you are irrationally jealous and controlling. A narcissist who is keeping you isolated may try to convince you that you are a paranoid and suspicious person. Gaslighting tactics are meant to make you feel crazy, so you attribute your legitimate concerns about the relationship to your own mental health issues rather than the other person's behavior.

Blaming the Victim

Gaslighting often goes hand in hand with blaming the victim. The abuser may accuse you of abusing them, or of somehow provoking their abusive behavior. The most common form of "blaming the victim" is seen in cases of domestic violence, where a partner hits you but then blames you for making them so angry in the first place.

In some cases, the narcissist can even convince other people that they really have been wronged and that their victim is "the real abuser." The narcissist's superficial charm can sometimes fool people, leading them to accept a twisted and one-sided interpretation of events. These people can then be manipulated into siding with the narcissist or participating in a smear campaign against the victim of the narcissist's abuse. Victims have coined the phrase "flying monkeys" to describe people who have been manipulated into helping a narcissistic abuser, just like the flying monkey soldiers of the wicked witch in The Wizard of Oz.

The Big Picture

Some actions are clearly and unambiguously abusive, such as hitting the other person. Far more often, a toxic relationship has many complex aspects to it, and it's not so easy to say whether a partner is intentionally unmannerly or not.

The big picture is what really matters. Abuse isn't about being passive-aggressive or guilt-trippy on a few occasions—it's an ongoing pattern of control and manipulation. The narcissist isn't just acting out in a moment of weakness but using you as a means to an end. That end is a deep need that can never be satisfied, and the roots of that need to go back to childhood.

Chapter 6 Learning The Language Of Narcissist: Who Abusers Use Anything And Everything Against Their Victims

If you do have to walk away from a narcissistic partner, friend, family member, etc., then there are a few things you need to know about 'after the event'.

It's this simple - a narcissist is not likely to shrug his or her shoulders and say, 'okay then, see you', and then let you walk away with nothing else occurring. It's far more likely that they will revert to their best behavior and try and lure you back.

There is one very good reason for this - because they hate rejection and take it very badly indeed. When you walk away from a narcissist you are rejecting them as a person, no matter how badly they treated you. They will not see all the emotional abuse and manipulation that came your way, in their eyes, they treated you like a king or queen. Instead, they will see you walking away, and it will rile them, or cut deep into their self-conscious depths. The next step could be one of two things:

- They will either become angry and resentful and probably bombard you with messages and social media posts about how they're better off without you and you're this, that, and the other (more abuse)

- Or they all become the epitome of charm once more and try and remind you of all the good times

If you find scenario one coming your way, ignore and block. This is simple pride getting in the way. In this case, they see you as rejecting them, they see you as making a mistake, and they're turning the whole thing on you. Of course, you know better. Block their number, block them on social media, do not go anywhere you know they will be, and go and stay with a friend for a while if you're worried, they're going to turn up at your door. Eventually, they will become bored and grow tired with no response. Sad, but true.

Scenario two is also common, and this is how many people in narcissistic relationships end up going back time and time again. The only answer here is to stand firm and remember why you left. If you can stick with your tried and tested support group, then even better. These people will remind you when your resolve might be wobbling, and it will at some point. You did have good times, and you were with them for a reason. Remember, if you've been a victim of gaslighting then it might also be that you're unsure of your next step because you're still suffering from the after-effects of this type of emotional abuse. Your friends and family will need to hold you firm in this case, but again, block numbers and social media access. The less they can contact you, the easier it will be for you to make large strides into your future.

What to Expect:

• Begging

• Pleading

• Bargaining

• Blame games

• Insults

• Eventual silence

If you think you're out of the woods then the silence comes, don't be so hasty. If they see you in the street quickly afterwards, bargaining and pleading is likely to start again. Breaking away from a narcissist takes time but know that it will be a process you'll be pleased you embarked on.

Dating After Leaving a Narcissist

Once you are over the 'getting away from a narcissist' process, the future will seem brighter and far clearer. It's important to give yourself the time to grieve the relationship properly, and not to jump straight into another union in order to try and block out the upset that occurred previously. This is a common scenario, but more common is trying to avoid another relationship altogether.

Remember that you cannot judge a future partner based on what you went through before, but it's entirely normal if you do.

For this reason, seeking out counseling or therapy after leaving a narcissistic partner is a good idea. By not dealing with everything that happened, you are actually putting your future at risk. Many people who have emerged from narcissistic relationships are so scarred by what they went through emotionally, they don't want to ever get close to another person again. As soon as a new partner starts to show even the tiniest hint of something which could be akin to narcissism, they run.

The fact is that we all show slight signs of narcissism from time to time, but that doesn't make us narcissists. We can all lack empathy sometimes, we can all belittle someone without meaning to once or twice, and we can all act in ways we wish we hadn't. The difference is that we will apologize and see the error of our ways, whilst a narcissist won't. Do not make the error of labelling everyone with the same tag or tarring everyone with the same brush.

The best way to dip your toe back into the dating world after emerging from a narcissistic relationship is to do so slowly. Try this:

• Give yourself time to simply be. Don't attempt to do anything, don't try and feel anything and don't push yourself to move on; simply spend time on yourself and try and unpick the events in your mind and deal with them. If you need to gain someone else's perspective, or you need to seek out professional help, now is the time to do so.

- Focus on yourself. Next, it's time to seek out things you enjoy and be kind to yourself. You spent so long with someone being unkind to you, it's likely that you've forgotten how to do things for yourself and to enjoy them. Find a hobby you've always wanted to try, go to a night class, go out with friends, spend Sunday mornings being lazy, read your favorite books, eat your favorite foods, and get out into nature.

- Focus on your health. Next up, after your self-focusing time, turn your attention to your health. A healthy body and mind are the best types of revenge! Whilst revenge shouldn't be on your mind, being a better version of yourself after a bad experience certainly feels great. Eat healthy foods, make sure you get plenty of exercise, get plenty of sleep, avoid stress, and make sure that you challenge your mind on a regular basis. You will notice how much stronger you feel.

- Enjoy your life. Once you start to feel better, and it may take considerable time in some cases, simply start to enjoy your life. Don't make it your sole aim to meet someone, and don't even think about dating; if it happens, it happens. There is plenty of time for all of that.

- When you're ready, simply be open to the possibility. The point is to try and meet someone who is worthy of your time and attention and who can give you what you didn't have before. The point isn't for someone to complete you or heal you. When you think you might be ready, simply be open to meeting people, but don't place huge importance on it. People who have come out of narcissistic relationships can sometimes be needy because they're so desperate for it not to happen again. By following these steps and placing importance on building yourself up once more, this is far less likely to happen to you.

- Do not tar them with the same brush. Again, if you do meet someone and you start to date, don't tar them with the same narcissistic brush as your ex. This is a vitally important step. True narcissists are very, very rare, and that is something to remember. It's highly unlikely you're going to meet someone with NPD twice in your lifetime, and whilst it's possible that you might meet someone who acts a little narcissistic on occasion, this isn't at rue narcissist and therefore won't bring the same types of problems.

- Know the signs. Do not run at the first sign of a problem but always hold your requirement for respect and understanding high up on your list. If someone starts to treat you badly, address the issue and stand firm before walking away. If being in a relationship with a narcissist will teach you anything, it's not to allow the same thing to happen again.

If you're reading this and thinking 'there's no way on Earth I'm even attempting to date again, I'm good by myself', it's time to question why you feel that way. Are you saying that because you truly don't want a relationship and you would rather be alone and spend your time traveling, making meaningful connections with friends, etc? Or, are you saying it because you're scared of going through the same thing twice?

Some people don't want to be in a relationship and that's fine, provided it's for the right reasons. If you're avoiding romantic connections simply because you're scared, that's something to address early on. You will probably find that your feelings change over time, but avoid being closed off to possible connections, simply because your past experiences are clouding your judgement.

Remember, you deserve to be loved, no matter what you might have been forced to believe in the past.

The Future for a Narcissist Who Refuses Help

We've talked a lot about the future for a person who was in a narcissistic relationship, but what about the future for the narcissist themselves?

It doesn't paint a great picture if the person isn't willing to seek help. In that case, it's far more likely that a narcissist will end up jumping from destructive relationship to destructive relationship, and if they do end up in a long-term union, it's unlikely that their partner will be truly happy and fulfilled. That person is far more likely to be simply 'putting up' with the narcissism.

If a narcissist ends up in a relationship which yields children, the sad truth is that their children are quite likely to develop narcissistic tendencies as a result of being open to them during their early years. Whilst there isn't a certain answer in terms of what causes NPD, there a definite suggestion that childhood experiences have a very firm link towards someone developing the personality development in their adolescent and then adult years.

Narcissists also have a habit of becoming quite bitter over time. This is partly because people have come into their lives and then left them, and they can't see why; of course, they will project the blame onto the other person and won't see their role in them leaving. Many narcissistic traits, therefore, worsen with age, as more experiences are racked up throughout life.

As you can see, it's quite a bleak picture we're painting and that is the sad truth about life as a narcissist. People will only stand being treated a certain way for so long before they eventually pluck up the courage to leave. Whilst some may never get to that point, these relationships are likely to be empty and lacking in true love and respect.

For these reasons, the biggest price a narcissist pays for their actions over time is loneliness and a lack of truly meaningful relationships in the end. For a narcissistic, however, the most loving and deep relationship they have is with themselves.

Are Modern Social Elements to Blame?

You're almost at the point where you know everything there is to know about Narcissistic Personality Disorder and the traits and issues which go alongside it, but we also need to explore one possible area before we sign off. Are modern social elements to blame for the rising number of narcissists in the world?

Remember, true narcissists are quite rare, yet it's a term that we hear on such a common basis. For that reason, perhaps narcissistic tendencies are becoming more common, and we have to question why that is. Is it down to the social pressures we are forced to deal with? Is it down to social media? Is it because of pressures to be the best, look the best, and own the best?

It's probably unfair to lay the blame of narcissism at the feet of modern society, but you have to wonder whether it has played a hand. For instance, social media has made us all so much more aware of other peoples' lives, and our appearances. Social media influences are always telling us that if we want to be the best, we need to look the best, and that means using this product. We're bombarded with people taking selfies and full body photos, without realizing that they've been photoshopped and filtered to within an inch of their lives. Most of what we see these days simply isn't real. Is it any wonder that we have such high and unrealistic expectations of what we're supposed to be, what we're supposed to look like, and what we're supposed to aim for?

We aren't entirely sure what causes NPD, so could it be the things we're exposed to in modern life? Of course, much of NPD is thought to be down childhood experiences, but what influences those experiences? What causes a person to act a certain way, causing trauma to another, which could then lead them to develop a specific type of personality disorder? It's hard to pinpoint, but you have to consider the possibility if nothing else.

Whilst we may never entirely understand what causes NPD, and there will always be a certain amount of stigma attached to it, trying to be the best is always a fruitless task. Perhaps instead we should simply be aiming to be ourselves.

In terms of future generations, perhaps it is our responsibility to ensure that children are raised to be happy with who they are, without the need to continually compete and reach certain unrealistic goals. By doing that, we will raise a generation of youngsters who are well-mannered, respectful of others and fulfilled. Surely those are major boosts towards avoiding personality disorders and the types of trauma which may contribute towards development.

Conclusion

And there we have it! We've reached the end of our book about narcissism, and by now you should be far clearer about what it is and what it really means.

After reading this book you should bandy around the idea of narcissism far less and appreciate that it is actually a truly rare personality disorder which shouldn't be misinterpreted. A person who is a little jealous or unkind once or twice in their life isn't a narcissist, they're simply having a bad day; provided they realize this and apologize to those they offended or hurt, there is no harm done. If however, that person doesn't see a problem with their actions, you could be dealing with someone who has an NPD touch.

Whilst a narcissistic cannot actually 'help' what they do, that doesn't mean that you should stick around and put up with it if they're not willing to seek out help to change. Leaving a narcissist behind isn't easy, but it is entirely necessary in order to live a happier life in the future.

The sad thing about narcissism is that whilst we're always talking about it in a negative way, the person who is truly affected is the narcissist themselves. This person is going to end up lonely unless they seek out steps towards a brighter future. This doesn't happen often however, because most narcissists don't realize there is anything wrong with them, and they assume that everyone else has the problem, not them.

Points to Take Away from This Book

Now you've read everything we've had to say about this rather confusing, yet fascinating subject, what are the main points to take away from the book?

• Narcissism is far rarer than most people think, with just 1% of the population affected on the whole

• True narcissism means being diagnosed with Narcissistic Personality Disorder (NPD)

• Men are far more likely to be narcissistic than women, however, that doesn't mean that female narcissist don't exist!

• A narcissistic is defined by a sense of the grandeur of one's self, inflated ego and self-importance, and a need to be the center of attention, but the traits are quite far-reaching beyond that

• Narcissistic behavior can be mild, moderate, or extremely severe

• Many narcissists use emotional abuse without even realize it, e.g. gas lighting

• There are several types of narcissists, including classic, vulnerable, and toxic

• Toxic or malignant narcissists are extremely damaging and are closely linked to psychopaths and sociopaths

- Many narcissists end up alone in the end, because they refuse to see a problem with their actions, and blame everything on those around them

- A person in a relationship with a narcissist is likely to be subjected to various levels of emotional abuse and manipulation, and will probably find it very hard to leave

- Empaths and narcissists are the worst combinations on the planet

- Treatment for Narcissistic Personality Disorder (NPD) involves therapy, counseling, behavioral therapy and challenging mindsets, and can take a considerable amount of time

- There is no known cause for NPD, however, it is thought to stem from childhood, and could be genetic

- Underneath it all, narcissists are fragile and lacking in self-confidence, with a need for constant validation

- Narcissists take rejection extremely badly

- In order for a person to receive treatment for NPD, they need to realize the problem for themselves, and this cannot be done for them. For this reason, most narcissists are never diagnosed and never treated

- It is impossible to fix or change a narcissist without them seeing the error of their ways and understanding that they have a personality disorder which requires treatment

- Finding the strength to leave a narcissistic relationship can be extremely difficult, and many people need to seek professional help afterwards, e.g. therapy and counseling

- Gaslighting is a very common tool employed by narcissists, which involves manipulating the thoughts and emotions of another person, causing them to question their own sanity

- You should never feel guilty or bad about needing to leave a narcissistic relationship - it's important to focus on yourself

There is a huge amount to talk about on this subject, and we've covered the main areas in detail, whilst reiterating the key points several times. Because narcissism and emotional abuse are so closely linked, this is a subject which requires a lot of press space. There is no fun in being in a relationship with a narcissist, just like there is no fun in a friendship with a narcissist or being closely linked in a working situation. All you will deal with is constantly belittling and their inflated sense of grandeur. Despite that, it's also important to realize that this person isn't a 'bad person', they're someone who is suffering from a personality disorder, which actually links very closely to other mental health problems.

By knowing all you can possibly know about narcissism, you can take the right steps towards managing a situation which is touched by narcissism in your own life.

The takeaway point from this whole book? If a narcissist tells you it's your fault, it's really not. Never feel guilty for putting yourself first.

Chapter 7 The Essential Dictionary To Understanding Narcissistic Abuse

Empathy is thus rather beneficial. However, in cases where an empath is not able to cope with all the feelings and emotions received and precepted from others, empathy may feel like a burden too heavy to withstand alone.

It may be easier for you to cope with what you are experiencing through empathy if you could first identify the type of empathy that defines you and describes you the best, even though empaths can have all of the three defined types.

Take a look at the types of empathy and try to find yourself in description and definition:

Cognitive Empathy

Cognitive empathy is strictly related to the theory of mind as referred to by psychologists and behavioralists. Cognitive empathy carries the ability to understand others by understanding their mental state and their mindset. Empaths that have increased cognitive empathy can somewhat predict what the other person would say based on understanding of their mind and their character. Cognitive empathy draws roots from the ability to deduct what the other person might say or think based on their previous "performance" as perceived by a cognitive empath. Psychologists refer to this social ability as to "thinking about thinking", where the empath with this ability is drawing conclusions on what the other person is thinking, or is capable of, based on determining their mindset, mental state, knowledge, emotions, desires, and even beliefs. It is not only that cognitive empathy allows you to guess what others might think or be able to do based on what you know about them, but it also allows you to understand why is that so – why is someone doing what they are doing based on all factors that you are able to perceive. Needless to say, cognitive empathy represents a rather valuable social skill.

The reason why cognitive empathy as a social skill is referred to as "the theory of mind" lies in the fact that as a person with strong cognitive empathy, you may only presume or predict what the other person would say or what is the other person thinking, or is able to do based on what you know about them and their personality, making it a theory more than a fact. Cognitive empathy is otherwise rather useful as a social skill as it may help you generate an appropriate social response based on what you are perceiving within your mind theory. Cognitive empathy is a rather crucial aspect of our social interaction as we are maturing and can be nurtured and improved already in the early age when your mind and emotions are yet to be defined and developed alongside your character and your personality. As we are growing up and maturing, the importance of understanding other people's mental state becomes very important in relation to how we are responding to other people's actions and reactions, as cognitive empathy helps us understand how someone's mental state may influence their actions. Resolving conflicts with other people also requires understanding how others might feel and how others may act based on their personality and various factors related to their mind and emotions.

Affective Empathy

Affective empathy is perhaps a type of empathy that may take the best out of an empath in case you are not sure how to respond to the way you are feeling about other people's emotions. The definition of affective empathy states that this type of empathy represents the ability to understand how others feel, so you can act in accordance with their emotions. This sensitivity can also backfire, as an empath who has increased affective empathy might be actually physically affected with what other people are feeling. While sympathy and compassion allow us to associate with other people and express our understanding for other people's emotions by being there for them and providing emotional and mental support, affective empathy actually affects empaths to feel the same way others do once they get emotionally involved. This state relates to the explanation we have previously provided on the topic of what empathy actually stands for, explaining the case as a product of emotional experiences that don't belong to us but can be mirrored by our brain receptors where the brain creates an emotional response to other people's distress the way it would generate an emotional reaction in case you would be the one going through that same situation someone else is going through. That is how affective empathy makes an empath feel the same way the other person does, while also carrying the ability to feel the emotions of others as their personal emotional distress. Still, affective empathy is yet another type of empathy that represents a social skill, as it allows us to feel concerned for other people based on the emotions we perceive.

Somatic Empathy

Somatic empathy, as you may guess by the name of this type of empathy, relates to actually feeling physical effects triggered by how you perceive that other people feel. With somatic empathy, the body of an empath may have a physical reaction to an emotion that other people are experiencing. For instance, as an empath who has increased somatic empathy, you may feel nervous when you notice that someone else feels the same way, or even when you know that the person you are connecting with is nervous about something. The same goes for any type of feeling – anger, sadness, disappointment, happiness – somatic empathy represents the ability to physically experience other people's emotions, which can also be rather overwhelming for empaths who are unable to control the way they are experiencing other people's emotions. The somatic nervous system will make the same response to other people's experiences just as it would be the case if you were the one going through that specific case, which is how somatic empathy is defined. Even though empathy represents an important social skill, regardless of which type of empathy is stronger, experiencing other people's emotions physically and emotionally may be exhausting for empaths who give in, or better said "feel in", which is the exact definition of the word "empathy" derived from the German word Einfühlung. Empathy as a term has been studied for around a century by far, however, the word empathy can also find its origins in the Greek word empatheia roughly translated to "in feeling".

How Can We Benefit from Empathy and Why Is It Important?

What needs to be understood is that empathy is indeed a crucial social skill and should be present in every human being – while some people may lack sympathy or compassion, being unable to care for others, these people can still have empathy and understand emotions – the only difference would be that they just don't care how others feel, which may lead to isolation and psychosocial deviations. We are after all social beings, which means that we rely on the company of others just as much we would be unable to survive without being connected to at least one person. Since early ages, when we are still growing up and learning, we also learn how to behave around other people and how to be able to generate an adequate social or emotional response when it is noted that there is a lack of appropriate reactions. For example, two children are playing and they are not getting along well because they both want the same toy at the same time – as they are yet growing up, they don't understand the concept of making compromises and may even have problems with sharing as little children are often acting selfishly. Both children are crying but neither of them is yet able to understand how the other well as their empathy is yet to be developed. This is where an adult has to balance everything and explain how the two children should act appropriately. However, there is an exception to every rule, so there are children whose character will allow them to empathize already in the early age even though social skills might not be entirely developed at that point. This type of children usually grows up to be highly sensitive to other people's emotions, which can sometimes be harmful for their own good.

Talking about the importance of empathy, you also need to note that some people may use their empathy as understanding how other people feel in order to manipulate those people, which is immoral the least to say, but is proving the fact that even people who are not compassionate and fail to sympathize with others can also have empathy. Empathy is thus a crucial part of the way we connect with others, as well as the way we connect.

The way we connect through empathy is actually a benefit that comes hand in hand with this social skill. Not only that people are able to empathize with others, but we can even experience emotions of fictional characters we see in movies and books, which allows us to experience emotions that we otherwise wouldn't be able to, making empathy an important part of emotional intelligence.

What is important to you to know as a highly sensitive being that has an increased capacity of feeling what other people feel, is that despite occasional hardships that may arrive with overreacting to what others are feeling, empathy is truly a gift. That gift allows us to be what we are born to be – human beings that can connect and coexist in a most poetic way – by feeling other people's emotions, which altogether describes the role and importance of empathy.

Precisely thanks to empathy, you are able to create bonds and healthy relationships with others, having the ability to connect on emotional level and to understand others as well as understand your own emotions and how these emotions affect your actions.

How Empathy May Affect Empath's Everyday Life?

Empathy, as we emphasized more than once, is a crucial social skill that helps us establish relationships with other people and connect by understanding our own emotions and other people's emotions. Being an empath is healthy and even necessary based on that definition. But, what about the case of overactive empathy?

How to tell if you are being overactive in empathizing to the extent where your empathy is affecting your everyday life in a negative way?

There are signs that you may pick up in your own reactions to other people's emotions by that may indicate that you might be an overactive empath, which may harm you mentally, spiritually and psychologically.

There are people who are sensitive to how others feel, which can sometimes go beyond their control, which is why protecting themselves from negative influence of other people's emotions comes in as a crucial point of survival. Since you have come this far with the book, you are probably having a hard time with balancing the effects that different people leave on you with their own emotional experiences that are easily soaked in by your sensitive nature. That is how empathy may affect your everyday life, leaving you stranded on how to protect yourself from negative effects that different emotional experiences may imprint on your own map of emotions.

Starting from feeling overwhelmed to actually being able to feel physically exhausted, the inability to control the effects that empathy may be leaving on you may make your life far more difficult to the point where overactive empathy feels like a curse, which is less likely the case with people who are able to balance the way they are receiving and perceiving different emotional experiences that don't originally belong to them.

The fact with overactive empathy is that it leaves the person affected by it vulnerable to other people's emotions making it difficult for an overactive empath to control the way these emotions are received and experienced. Whenever you, as an empath, receive a combination of emotions or a strong emotional reaction appearing at other people, you actually become open to the effects of these emotions. In case you are able to balance this emotional reaction and your response to it, you can use your sensitivity in form of empathy to help others by understanding them, that way also creating bonds and significant relationships. However, in cases where you are more likely to give in to overactive empathy, your emotions are being directed towards the other person with a purpose of helping them feel better, while you are receiving and keeping negative emotions. Overactive empaths may flourish in the presence of love, joy, happiness and positive emotions, as well as among people who know how to appreciate their sensitivity. However, in case an empath with increased sensitivity is exposed to people who may take advantage of their empathy and sensitivity, an empath may feel exhausted, tired, depressed, and even physically ill.

This sort of environment may cause you to retreat and become an introvert as an overactive empath as you would want to avoid the feeling of despair and fatigue that other people may leave on you with negative emotions.

Another case scenario that may affect your life in a negative way is feeling empathy and giving out your positive energy to people who do not deserve to be empathized with. Let's face it – as much as there are people with empathy who want to help others, there are manipulative people capable of horrible feelings, and perhaps worse – horrible actions and reactions. As an empath, you need to try and distance yourself from toxic environments in order to be able to balance emotions you are picking up with your own emotional response, and we are going to show you how this can be done further in the book.

Empaths with overactive empathy also tend to take over other people's problems alongside their emotions which is because empathy allows us to feel the need to help others and feel compassion for problems that aren't even ours to solve. Helping others is a wonderful thing that connects us with other people, but in case you don't own your empathy and the empathy owns you, you won't be able to distance yourself from completely taking over the problems of others. Without boundaries between your own life and other people's lives, you may become easily overwhelmed and even neglect your own problems, which over time becomes debilitating for your personal life.

Even though you are blessed with overactive empathy, that doesn't mean that you should throw your life away and focus on everyone else's feelings and problems but yours. Overactive empathy may also turn your relationships upside down and lead to codependence, making the way you are connecting with others unhealthy for you. Without setting up boundaries between you and the people you care for, you are preventing them from facing their problems on their own, taking over the role of bringing change into other people's lives instead of allowing them to make changes by themselves with a little push from your side. These sorts of scenarios may create a rather unhealthy environment for you as a highly sensitive person, while your emotional involvement will definitely take its toll over time.

Empaths who have problems with balancing their sensitivity may also be suppressed to energy drainage as you can easily be pulled into feeling other people more than you feel yourself. If you are investing yourself in others, who is investing in your own emotional state?

It may be the case that you are also able to pick up the atmosphere from different places and allow this experience to overwhelm you. Has it ever happened to you that you just walk into a building, come to a visit to someone's house, or pay a visit to someone at a hospital and you can just feel that something isn't quite right? You may feel anxious, sad, and even uncomfortable and scared in case you allow these settings to overwhelm you.

In some cases, empaths may feel physical distress such as headache, nausea, and develop problems of addictions to food alcohol and even drugs as a way of helping themselves cope with what they are going through, while other people's emotions would continue to take more from their sensitivity.

There are so many factors that can affect the quality of your life in case you don't learn how to set boundaries and control the way you feel about different emotions, places, energies and people, which is why we will try and teach you how to avoid falling in despair and gaining control over what you feel.

Is Empathy a Weakness?

In our culture, sensitivity may be considered to be a flaw, and the sad truth is not different when it comes to natural selection – the strongest survive. However, empathy and the sensitivity to other people's emotions doesn't need to be a weakness even though your empathy may at times feel like you have your own kryptonite set to bring your weaknesses at once when faced to it. The sad truth also lies in the case that most parents, if the choice would be narrowed down to only "this or that" would choose their child to be a bully rather than be bullied, and we all know who among the two has more empathy for how others feel. Evolution through natural selection demands from us to be strong – it's a requirement even, and that doesn't only include physical strength, but mental as well. However, you need to know that in the modern age where our evolution comes down to curing diseases that were once deadly, increasing life span and correcting weaknesses given by nature, sensitivity might not be viewed upon as a weakness – but rather as a crucial skill to connect with people and understand them. With social media booming and communities growing, connecting with people becomes more important, not only for emotional reasons, but also for practical purposes such as working and cooperating together, exchanging thoughts and opinions, as well as making friends and starting relationships. Empathy may be a true gift in these cases for empaths who know how to control the way other people's emotions are affecting them. In case you allow different energies and emotions that don't actually belong to you, to put you in a state of distress and make you feel isolated and over the edge, your empathy may be viewed as a weakness, but once you learn how to control what you feel, your sensitivity in form of empathy becomes your strength that may open many doors for you.

Now that you have learned the basics on what exactly means to be increasingly empathetic and sensitive to emotions and energies around you, we are set to show you some valuable techniques on how to protect yourself and use your empathy as an advantage, while adopting techniques that will help you heal emotionally, spiritually and psychologically.

Chapter 8 Dating Emotional Predators

By this point in our journey to better understand narcissistic individuals, one thing should be crystal-clear: there is no chance for a long-term relationship with a person that has NPD. Any "love story" with such individual will end up with heartbreak, shattered dreams, and maybe even years of your life wasted away.

Even when the victim is held tightly in the narcissist's grasps and is forced to accept the reality that he/she wants, deep down, they are aware of the hopeless situation they are in. No matter how hard you might try to deny the truth and rationalize the actions of a narcissist, in the end, it all boils down to the fact that you fell in love with someone that never existed. A charming, wonderful person that promised you the moon and the stars, and you, a kind-hearted individual with a lot of love in your heart to give, trusted him/her. The reality that your soulmate was "fabricated" by a sick, malicious person is absolutely mind-shattering and heartbreaking, for anyone that has to go through it. The trauma eats you up from the inside, even months after the relationship has ended, and the experience changes you in ways you never knew were possible.

No matter how strong-willed, independent, confident someone was before entering into a relationship with a narcissist, the experience steals all of these good things away from you, reducing you to a shadow of your old self, an empty shell that feels hopeless. Not even celebrities are safe from the grasp of abusive relationships. Reese Witherspoon admitted in an interview with Oprah, to have been involved in an emotionally abusive relationship at a young age, also adding that leaving the said relationship was the hardest decision she ever had to make. Stacey Solomon, the presenter of Loose Women, has as well been outspoken about her abusive experience, going as far as describing on the program how it changed her, "I was in an abusive relationship, and it makes you forget who you are. It made me feel like I'd never be the same person again. No matter what I do, I'll always be this weird version of myself. A part of me does begrudge that person for taking that away from me. If someone says something over and over again, it can embed in you."

Another famous example, that might come as a surprise, is actor Johnny Depp. He was in a physically and emotionally abusive relationship with actress Amber Hart, but, because our society is biased to believe that only men can be abusers, people believed his now ex-wife's lies, and he was blamed for months of being the perpetrator. Hart used his fame and money to propel herself up, and even proudly advocated as a member of the #MeToo movement. It took several hours of video evidence, multiple witnesses, hospital bills, domestic violence reports, and even Hart herself confessing to attacking her partner in two instances, to make the public accept the fact that Depp was the victim all along.

So, to reiterate my point, abuse can happen to anyone, regardless of gender or popularity. Nothing makes us immune in this world filled with wolves in sheep's clothing. It sounds scary and hard to accept, but this is the reality of it. You are not at fault for putting your trust in a mentally deranged person, because you had no way of knowing their real self at the time. And when you did start noticing the truth, you were already strapped in the horror ride of your life, with little to no way out in sight.

Unfortunately, the only way to put an end to narcissistic abuse is for the victim to initiate the break-up, as soon as he/she realizes that their partner is a narcissist. Break-ups take a lot of time, resilience, strength, effort, will-power, and support. It will take every single bit of energy that you may have left, after the constant abuse in your relationship, and, even when the break-up is done, the effective escape is only halfway done. Keep in mind that victims are emotionally and psychologically addicted to their partners and thus, very vulnerable to hoovering attempts. You may have to go through this 'break-up' 20 odd times until you build up the strength necessary to reject any reconciliation attempts. As time goes by, you will become more and more powerful. However, the only way in which you can break-off the control that the narcissist has over you is by adopting a No-Contact stance (or a low/limited contact if that's not possible).

No-Contact is the only solution that prevents relapse into the abusive, intoxicating relationship, and it is the first real step towards getting back control over your life. Think of a relationship with a narcissist as an addiction. You know that it's toxic and harmful. Even if it provides pleasures (in this case small episodes of "love" that makes you feel validated), a long-term relationship could ruin you and destroy you as a person. You realize that it needs to stop, but addiction messes with our brain in such a way that it is very hard to put an end to it. And in order to escape that addiction, you need to stay free of that toxic substance that your brain craves, or in this case, that toxic person. That's why No-Contact should be your first step. Your mind and body need to "detox" in order to truly start healing. Every contact you have with the narcissist, post-breakup, is equivalent to you taking in a small quantity of that "drug" back into your system, which is why the danger to "relapse" is so high in these situations. That little dose will have you wanting more, and after a long, emotionally draining fight to leave them, you will have to fight again, and again to make sure that you stay on the right track.

One of the most challenging types of relationships to end is one with a narcissist, and there are numerous reasons for this. For many individuals, the kindness, loyalty, and desire to keep the promises they have made along the line, make it extremely difficult to do so. The narcissist can also make leaving a problematic process because he wants to be the one to call the shots in the relationship, including when it has to do with ending it. So long as the victim believes keeping the relationship going is a vital element to their lives, the narcissist will have the freedom to control them and the choices they make.

For many individuals in a relationship with a narcissist, the breaking point is when the narcissist performs a specific action that they won't tolerate. However, for many victims, this breaking point differs. However, male victims of a narcissistic relationship are not as likely to leave in comparison to female victims. This may be due to the additional weight of responsibility culturally felt by men to see to the needs of women.

Notwithstanding, when a victim of a narcissistic relationship does take the step to leave, they find it hard to stick to the choice they made. This is mostly a result of pity and guilt they feel for the narcissist. Besides, if the narcissist fails to let the victim leave, they will continuously pressure the victim to have a change of heart, frequently with the typical promise to change and do better, which is often not true. The narcissist can make the life of the victim trying to leave the relationship very stressful so as to keep dominating them alongside the relationship.

Do Narcissists Ever End the Relationship First?

There are situations where a particular circumstance will urge the narcissist to end the relationship. These may include events which change the way life is for either the narcissist or the victim. If the victim falls severely sick, unable to move or not able or willing to go on with the life that has been created by the narcissist any longer, this may urge the narcissist to end the relationship. There are times where good events like having a new kid can change the power dynamics in the relationship. This is common in instances where the narcissist has to show more empathy or become more responsible. Some factors that can make the narcissist end the relationship abruptly with a victim include loss of a job, old age, illness, or a promotion at work.

However, for many victims, the narcissist never leaves and sticks like glue, continuing to dominate the victim as he or she so pleases. How then do you leave the relationship in this instance? Below, we will be looking into a few helpful things that can help make this process a seamless one.

Complete Detachment

The first step, of course, will be to end the relationship, and once you do this, you need to ensure you do not remain in contact. This is extremely crucial because, at this point, you are still in search of closure and want answers to what went wrong.

This applies even if you know deep down that no response will arise, and this individual still makes you vulnerable.

You need to remember how you found yourself in the position you are in the first place. Do not put yourself through the process of abuse and incessant pain once again. You need to behave like this individual is not on the same planet as you, which in a way is correct. The individual you are yearning for now is only a smokescreen. Stick to that and make sure you keep them closed out totally.

The narcissist will certainly make efforts to reach out by every means possible. Block their numbers and divert all emails to the junk folder. You need to ensure they do not have access to you at their bidding anymore, as the narcissist will try everything possible to get you back.

If there are kids in the equation, you may need to get the help of a third party who will act as an intermediary if you can. If this is not possible, remember to exercise caution and never meet up by yourself with the narcissist you just barely escaped from. You can get the assistance of a qualified therapist to help you put a parenting plan in place. This is a document which is legally binding and has information about financial responsibilities, time-sharing for the kids, and means of reaching out allowed by both parties involved. This can further help ease the process.

Unfriend Mutual Friends

A friend of your narcissistic partner may not be aware of his lifestyle, and they may tell you that you're making a mistake by leaving him. They'll begin to tell you all he has accomplished and why you should have stayed. To prevent hearing about your partner and how he's doing, cut ties with anyone that keeps discussing him even after you made it clear you don't want to hear anything about them. Unfriend them to keep your sanity and if possible, go somewhere far. Narcissists are very good at persuasion and pretense, and they can send a close friend to make you change your mind, knowing the friend does not know them as much as you do.

Write Down the Things that Made You Leave

Due to the deceitful nature of narcissists, you may find yourself reminiscing on the good times you spent with them. This is why you need always to remember the bad times too. The times that the narcissist made you feel worthless and guilty about what he's supposed to be blamed for.

Remember the times that they made you cut ties with your family and the times you question your sanity because you believed you were going crazy. Most notably, remember when you were manipulated and lied to even when you knew it was all lies, and the narcissist told you it was your mind playing tricks on you. Put all these down in a diary and keep safe.

Whenever you start remembering the good times in the relationship, get the journal, and read it.

Remember That Narcissists Heal in a Short Period

Narcissists are very good at getting someone new as soon as you leave. They do not waste time before healing from breakups, and sometimes, they already have a preplanned exit strategy. This is how the narcissists believe they can win the game - since the relationship is a game to them.

Avoid Being Tempted to Stay

Narcissists always try to win back their victim by telling them sweet things. They'll leverage on the fact that they're aware of your weaknesses and use this to sweet talk you into coming back to them. Spend time alone and have a serious reflection about past events. This will enable you to understand yourself better, and you'll recognize any form of deceit when you see it.

Avoid being coerced into changing your mind, as narcissists are very good at coercion. They'll tell you what you want to hear at that moment, but it's all part of their game plan. As soon as you accept and go back to them, be ready for another dose of mistreatment, abuse, and emotional blackmail. It's best not to bother going back when you leave, even if you need to pick an essential item you left behind. If you must visit again, do so with caution and don't be deceived by the kind words you'll hear. Ensure you let them know you've moved on and they should do the same. Wish them the best and block their number. If you can't face them because you're not sure of yourself, do it by calling or texting them.

A narcissist will try everything possible to convince you that you have made a grave mistake by attempting to leave them. You may have developed a kind of disbelief in yourself after many months or years of being with a narcissist. They try to persuade or intimidate you to get back to them by telling you to remember the good times and the good things you've done together. They blackmail you emotionally by telling you that you're overreacting and stressing them. They even tell you that you only see the negativities without looking at the positive side.

Even though they may try to let you see the positive aspects of the relationship and why you should stay, they'll always blame you and tell you you're the one with a problem. They'll manipulate you into believing you're doing the wrong things and not helping the relationship. If you're not strong enough, you'll discover that you're losing your self-esteem and the only option you think of is staying. If they find it difficult to persuade you, they'll start talking about your negative sides to devalue you and make you feel bad. They'd start by telling you how you would have amounted to nothing if you hadn't met them, how poor you were before you met them, how you'll suffer if you leave them and how successful they'll be when you leave. They'll also let you know that finding someone that will really love them and put them first is straightforward. If they still need you, they won't want you to disrupt their plans as leaving them means they can no longer control you as you have more power in the relationship.

Forgive a Narcissistic Partner or Friend

Rather than feelings of hatred and anger towards a narcissist, look beyond the picture and understand that narcissism is a disorder. A narcissist is a weak person who devalues, degrades, and abuses their target to fill a void. Understanding this will enable you to leave a narcissistic person in peace without further drama. You can then easily forgive them and forgive yourself. Quit blaming yourself, as narcissists are known to be perfect manipulators and it's challenging to differentiate between reality and illusion when you're dealing with them. Yes, they're that good!

Take Time to Heal and Grieve

Yes, you need time to heal completely and grieve about who you thought your partner was. As soon as the narcissist's schemes aren't working again, you're able to really know the person you're dealing with. It may come to you as a big shock because of the kindness and affection shown to you at the early stage of your relationship. By the time you become attached and form an emotional bond with this person, you've already gone far into the relationship. However, always thank yourself and be proud of yourself for taking the bold step by leaving because the emotional abuse would have been worse if you remained with them.

Get Busy

Keeping yourself busy will help you heal faster and move on with your life. If you're not sure of what to do, you can write down a list of exciting things to do and get yourself occupied with this. You can exercise, take a walk, visit the zoo, go on a tour, learn something new or anything that makes you happy. Strive to get better at what you do and learn more. Grow as you learn and concentrate on things that'll make you happy. Ensure you move with people that share the same views and ideas with you. You can join groups on social media platforms to make this easier.

Concentrate on the Future

As soon as you leave a narcissistic person, it is essential that you concentrate on positive thoughts and energy on doing great things for yourself and the people around you. Forget the past and focus more on the present. Thoughts of how to be a better you and heal faster should be your major focus at this point.

Love Yourself

You must have suffered lots of emotional trauma by living with a narcissist for months or years, and you may even have concluded that you don't deserve to be loved. That's what the narcissist has planned, and you shouldn't let it happen. Be kind to yourself and love yourself. Once you do everything to ensure you love yourself, any other person that comes your way will have to reciprocate. Self-love will help you build confidence in yourself and find love again. Don't flog yourself for too long, and ensure you always set proper boundaries.

Believe in Yourself

From time to time, you may find yourself thinking about your experience in the relationship, trying to figure out where you went wrong. This is not right! No one deserves to be mistreated as you were. Don't try to justify their actions. Believe in yourself and know the right thing for you. With time, you'll understand that you deserve a lot better than being stuck in a relationship with a narcissist. You'll regain your self-esteem and have a true understanding of who you are. Soon, you'll be compassionate to yourself and move on to healthy and happy relationships.

It would seem counterintuitive for anyone to want to be with someone who is concerned only with him or herself.

We seek romance and relationships in order to receive validation among other things companionship brings. There are hormones involved that will draw two people together and bind them in a whirlwind of emotions and positive vibes. It is supposed to be reciprocal with lots of give and take.

So it is kind of strange at first blush to see how it would be possible to strike that sort of balance with a narcissist. The incessant need for validating the other person while receiving nothing on the other end would be, to put it mildly, emotionally and physically exhausting. To live in the long shadow of a person who demands attention and will subjugate you to the shadows without a second thought.

Here is how it makes sense. Narcissists have a few things going for them, especially at the beginning of a new relationship.

They are very charming, they enjoy the attention, and they have a lot of charisma. All of this sucks people in to them and causes them to want to be around them. According to Susan Whitbourne at Psychology Today this is very common. She compares it to a chocolate cake, where eating just a little bit is fun and satisfying but eating an entire cake everyday can give you diabetes and heart disease.

Narcissists will make you feel like you are the center of their world. You will be convinced this person wants to marry you and spend their life with you through thick and thin.

This is of course and by nature a very short lived but intense experience. This is not happening because they are so attracted to you, although they may believe it at the time. No, the need is different. This is their way of causing you to need them, to validate them, to admire and adore them.

What is happening is called love bombing. The constant showering of attention and validation leading to the inevitable step of them pulling away and causing you to now need them like a drug. It really is like a drug too. The narcissist was giving freely now the source is gone and the person so used to being showered with attention and in the process getting a little dopamine tick each time is now fiending for more.

Do you want to know if you are in a relationship with a narcissist before it is too late?

Chapter 9 The Narcissistic Translator

Narcissists everywhere have similar taste in targets. Because they almost universally rely on manipulation tactics that follow specific patterns, they also tend to seek out the same kinds of people because those tactics work on those people. Certain traits can make for a particularly attractive target for narcissistic abuse, and if you have all five of the ones that are listed, you may find yourself desired by narcissists around you, seeking you out and wanting to abuse your good nature in order to meet their own narcissistic supply. Recognize that not all of the traits listed here are necessarily negative or bad to have, but when combined, they do leave you vulnerable. Understanding which of these traits you may have will help you better protect from narcissistic traps.

Desirable or Attractive Traits or Possessions

Since narcissists only think about themselves, they are only ever doing things if they want something. It could be money, power, status, or attractive partners, or anything else. Regardless of what the narcissist desires, if she finds someone who has what she wants, she will want to pursue a further relationship with him or her. Attracting a narcissist's attention means you have something that the narcissist values and that are the first criteria to being a narcissist's victim. Even if you do not meet the rest of the criteria on this list, just having something desirable means that the narcissist will be more inclined to try to get close to you just to mirror and emulate you. After all, she might be able to get what you have if she acts just like you.

Caregiver

Some people naturally gravitate toward caring for others. They are frequently very empathetic and loving, and their empathy makes them compassionate towards others and their struggles. Because of that compassion and empathy, these people are more inclined to help others in any way they can, even if that involves plenty of patience and understanding, even if some pain is expected along the way.

That compassion, empathy, and patience that caregiver types exhibit is incredibly attractive to narcissists. Narcissists crave attention and admiration, and someone with a caregiver personality is quite likely to happily provide the kind of attention a narcissist needs in the name of taking care of him or her. Knowing that narcissists actively seek out compassionate individuals who thrive on caring for others because they know that these people will see the narcissist as someone in dire need of caring and compassion. They will regard the narcissist with more grace than could ever be deserved and do everything they can to meet the narcissist's needs.

Grew up with Dysfunction

Dysfunctional upbringings cause people to develop skewed senses for what is and is not normal. People often default to what they grew up with as the norm and often repeat what was seen in childhood. When you grow up in a dysfunctional household, you fail to see the glaring red flags around you in the future. For example, if you grew up seeing people who disrespect each other, you normalize that and when you find yourself being sworn at by a narcissist, it seems normal to you. You do not realize that, in healthy relationships, people do not swear at each other or call each other names when the only relationships that were ever modeled for you involved those behaviors. You do not learn to set up normal, healthy boundaries because the people you grew up around failed to set them.

When you have had that dysfunctional way of life modeled and normalized for you, you are far more likely to accept those abusive tendencies in the future simply because you do not know better. Accepting those behaviors for someone you love is an acceptable compromise when you have never seen any different, and because of that, you are an easy target. Because you lack proper boundaries or a proper idea of what a normal relationship is like when you grow up in a dysfunctional home, you are far more likely to seek out something familiar, even if familiar is unhealthy.

Avoids Confrontation

Narcissists are able to get away with their behaviors because oftentimes, those around them are confrontation avoidant. Since the manipulation tactics a narcissist frequently employs require manipulation, which requires the narcissist to avoid being called out in order to work, narcissists tend to gravitate toward people who are uncomfortable with conflict. These people are far more likely to submit and give the narcissist whatever she may desire in the name of avoiding conflict, which works just fine for the narcissist. She wants to find people who will tolerate her manipulation and abuse, even if that tolerance is hesitant or faked. Since, by nature, no confrontational people avoid arguments, they tend to shy away from calling out manipulation or inconsistencies as they happen, and they are likely to tolerate being mistreated because putting up with the manipulation and abuse is seen as more tolerable than creating a conflict. Unfortunately, though no confrontational individuals attempt to avoid conflict at all costs, their peaceful nature has a tendency to attract the attention of those who would love nothing more than to abuse that peacefulness for their own personal gain.

Lacking Self-Esteem

People with low or virtually nonexistent self-esteem crave love and affection. They want to feel special or as though someone loves them, even though they simultaneously feel as though they are worthless or unworthy for some reason. Their low self-esteem leaves them feeling as though they are unimportant or less deserving of success, happiness, love, and family; though these may be the things they crave more than anything else.

Because people with low self-esteem crave that connection and love more than anything, they will frequently put up with abuse because they think it is the only way they will ever receive it. Even though every person is deserving of love, people with low self-esteem do not believe this. This leaves them vulnerable, as when they do find someone who takes a special interest in them, they are willing to go along with anything. Those with low self-esteem are more susceptible to the love-bombing stage, and will likely cling to any scraps of perceived affection, even if they come with abuse and negativity. Due to feeling as though no one else could love them because of their perceived faults, they are willing to put up with the abuse of the one person they believe will. Because of that willingness to put up with the abuse, narcissists seek those with low self-esteem out, knowing they will be able to be manipulated into believing that the controlling behaviors are an attempt at showing love and are proof that the narcissist loves them. Those with low self-esteem may even believe that the harsh criticisms are true and that the narcissist is actually trying to help correct for those flaws in order to help them grow into the person they ought to be. Unfortunately, that could not be further from the truth, and the narcissist only seeks to keep self-esteem at an all-time low for ease of manipulation.

Chapter 10 Have A Love Affair With Yourself?

You have been in a relationship with a narcissist for years, and that has left you scarred, scared witless, and feeling unlovable. In your mind, you believe you don't deserve to be happy because that is what your narcissist ex had told you all the time.

You are feeling numb, and the pain is eating at you. Let me just ask, "Are you a giver? Do you believe that it is better to give than to receive?" That is all and good for you, but what happens when you have nothing left to give?

When you have given everything, and you are down to nothing, having a love affair with yourself is the way to heal.

Get to Know Yourself

Self-appreciation starts with getting to know yourself. Acknowledge your thoughts, feelings, and emotions, as well as your fears and fantasies. It is great to spend time with friends and family, but don't forget to have some quality time with just you.

Many of us today are addicted to our phones, computers, and TV. Some of us even more addicted to our work. When you are on your alone time, turn these gadgets off to have time off from digital noises. Why don't you spend this time writing in your journal instead?

While doing that, it will be relaxing to listen to your favorite music. Of course, it is okay if you just want to savor the silence. Get to know yourself by clearing your mind of the chatter. Take a deep breath and let your mind wander where it wants to go. Instead of doing, focus on simply being.

Engage in Self-Expression

After losing yourself to narcissistic abuse, we often forget the things we used to like. You can revisit or recover these hobbies by engaging in some self-expressing activities. Doing so helps you connect with inner self and achieve a higher nature of being.

Some self-expression projects you can do include yoga, meditation, dance, or singing. You can also go for a walk, swim, run, or bike ride. Writing a journal is also a form of self-expression. Sometimes, just even laughing out loud or having a good cry is good for your soul.

Treat Yourself with Kindness

The best thing you can do for self-love is to be kind to yourself. Even when you have screwed up so many times in your life, be patient. Criticizing yourself will never change a thing. It only results in you doubting yourself even more and adopting a negative attitude.

Don't shy away from complimenting yourself. Helping others is also a way to treat yourself with kindness. The warm feelings of seeing the smiles of other people you have helped are a fantastic way of countering the self-doubt. This way, you can confidently love yourself.

Pamper Yourself from Time to Time

Part of having a love affair with yourself is pampering and courting yourself. From time to time, it is okay to indulge in aesthetic enjoyment, such as activities for sensory delight. It feels good as well to have all your favorite colors, sounds, smells, and textures surround you as part of self-expression.

Pampering yourself also includes getting dressed up from time to time just for the fun of it. You can take yourself on a dream date and reward yourself with special treats. Get a massage or dance until you drop. Most importantly, tell yourself, "I love you" every day.

Performing these practices are meant to ensure that you don't feel obliged to be with someone for fear of loneliness or desperation. When you know your worth and are never short of showing self-love, no one can make you feel like you are not enough. Because you are and you deserve nothing but the best.

Conclusion

You have by now been able to understand the roles that partners take on in any relationship. You now know yourself as a narcissist or a codependent, or otherwise and interdependent partner. If you are a narcissist, you are now aware of your proneness for power and likely addictions, which are actually in control of you, and not you controlling them. For the codependent you are now aware of your tendencies avoid responsibility of yourself for other people.

Everyone desires for a perfect relationship. But this is not attained in principle alone. It takes effort. The human magnet syndrome has revealed to you how you might have ended up in your relationship without due consideration. But you have also gained helpful insights on how to rectify your behaviors and lead your relationships in a conscious manner in order to bring it to the standards you wish for yourself and your loved one.

Narcissism and codependence do not just erupt in adulthood. These are behaviors that are one adapts to from childhood. Childhood emotional negligence is discussed, and strategies for overcoming its effects explained in adequate detail. These attachment styles occur in different relationship types, but the similarities and differences in each have been explored. Narcissists exhibit self-centeredness in their desires, but so do codependences, though they may seem to have a different disposition on the surface.

A narcissist and a codependent can, however co-exist. This is explained in the healing processes and explaining how you can understand your partner of a different attachment style from your own, and how you can adjust your behaviors to accommodate and probably improve your partner's values and personality. This is explained in the healing process. With commitment from all parties, relationships can become ideal as desired by members. You now know how an ideal relationship works.

Emotional abusers are not going to let go, because there is still the psychic cord between you and the abuser. The invisible rope stops you from getting involved with the narcissist even after the relationship is over.

Because of this relation, you will feel several different and negative emotions. This can lead to a lot of frustration and conflicting emotions such as indignation or disappointment, remorse, rage, and even unfaithfulness. It can be much easier to recover from this form of chronic suffering if you know where to start the healing process.

Emotional abuse is a form of behavioral control, but you can free yourself from this type of suffering. If you have endured any kind of violence, you might not have shown your real feelings because of your lack of emotional maturity. You may still depend on an individual to meet your moving needs.

You must trust that you can meet your emotional needs. You don't have to look endlessly to others to show that you are cherished. Remember that the emotional abusers who won't let go can be solved.

One must bear in mind that narcissism is a mental disorder. We won't change, even if you help them stop abusing themselves and feeling something is wrong. Remove any thoughts you can and will help a narcissist absolutely.

The best thing you can do is to respect yourself and to know how to live unreliably. This will restore your trust and respect for yourself. You're really responsible for your thoughts.

Keep in mind that you will never be able to make a narcissist happy because they lack self-confidence deep inside. You feel good about yourself only if you are hurt in some way.

Remember also that a narcissist wants to control you and will not let you go smoothly. The irony is that they believe, like you, that they are betrayed and abandoned.

You have to wake up and understand what love really means. The good news is that you can get plenty of support for such a destructive relationship that clearly consumes your soul.